*The* **NASCAR**
*FAMILY ALBUM*

# The NASCAR

## FAMILY ALBUM

### STORIES AND MEMENTOS FROM AMERICA'S MOST FAMOUS RACING FAMILIES

BY H. A. BRANHAM

CHRONICLE BOOKS
SAN FRANCISCO

This edition published in 2007 by Chronicle Books LLC.

*The NASCAR Family Album* is produced by becker&mayer!, LLC, Bellevue, Washington. www.beckermayer.com.

NASCAR is a registered trademark of the National Association for Stock Car Auto Racing.

Library of Congress Control Number: 2006906082

ISBN-10: 1-932855-58-0

ISBN-13: 978-1-932855-58-6

NASCAR Publishing:

Jennifer White

H. A. Branham

Emily Ross

Heather Greene

Manufactured in China

Design: Megan Noller Holt and Henry Quiroga
Editorial: Brian Arundel
Image Coordination: Shayna Ian and Lisa Metzger
Production Coordination: Nick Boone-Lutz
Project Management: Sheila Kamuda

10 9 8 7 6 5 4 3 2

Chronicle Books LLC
680 Second Street
San Francisco, CA 94107
www.chroniclebooks.com

Officially licensed by

Table of Contents

# *Foreword*

MY JOB AS CHAIRMAN AND CEO OF NASCAR IS CHALLENGING—AND REWARDING. IT'S also been a bit humbling at times. After all, I'm following in the footsteps of not one, but two men who left their own undeniable mark on the sport of stock car racing—my grandfather, William Henry Getty France, and my father, William Clifton France, or Bill Sr. and Bill Jr., as they're known to most people.

It's been said that Bill Sr. was responsible for creating NASCAR, and Bill Jr. was responsible for growing NASCAR. That's a pretty fair assessment I'd say, but it's definitely an abridged assessment. You could write an entire book—or several books—on how each of them went about their respective agendas.

Suffice it to say that there are some fundamental concepts they established that have helped define NASCAR, and the role of the France family.

First and foremost, I think you could say we always try to take a long-range, overall view of our sport when making decisions. No matter what the current impact—positive or negative—of a decision, we always try to look down the road, to completely evaluate how a decision might shake out in the long run. Which makes sense. Seldom are situations as good or as bad as they initially seem.

We have always tried to develop a business model where everybody benefits—drivers, owners, teams, tracks, sponsors, business partners, and of course, fans.

We have always tried to establish fairness as the defining, critical issue in the way we conduct NASCAR's business.

Overall, I think it's safe to say that the ideas—and *ideals*—of Bill Sr. and Bill Jr. have served as great guideposts for NASCAR. I know they've served me well. And I can't truly describe what a luxury it is for me to be able to walk down the hall of our offices in Daytona Beach, and seek the counsel of my father, who still serves NASCAR well as vice chairman. My uncle Jim, NASCAR's executive vice president, is a great help, as is my sister, Lesa Kennedy, also a vice president. And of course, my mother, Betty Jane, NASCAR's assistant secretary, is always there, offering guidance.

There are so many things for our family to take pride in regarding NASCAR's exponential growth in recent years. But perhaps the thing we're most proud of is the fact that NASCAR remains a family-oriented sport, both in the garage area and in the grandstands.

The book illustrates that family tradition, with its vast assortment of stories, stats, photos, and memorabilia. I hope you enjoy it—with your family.

Regards,

Brian Z. France

Bill France Sr. prepares to hold a driver's meeting before a NASCAR event at a Southeastern dirt track, circa 1952.

**CLOCKWISE FROM LOWER LEFT:** Rusty and Kenny Wallace; Dale Sr. and Dale Jr. Earnhardt; Bill Sr. and Anne France; David and Ricky Pearson; Darrell and Michael Waltrip; Ned Jarrett surrounded by family; Bobby (center) and Davey (left) Allison; Bobby, Bob, and Terry Labonte.

# Introduction

THE BURGEONING APPEAL OF NASCAR, THE NATIONAL ASSOCIATION FOR Stock Car Auto Racing, is a veritable cultural phenomenon. NASCAR is by far the fastest growing sport in the United States, as an ever-expanding and fiercely loyal television audience has rapidly embraced the adrenaline rush of drivers racing cars, inches apart, around tracks at breakneck speeds.

But as the sport has evolved from a Southeastern curiosity to blockbuster national television deals, one thing has remained the same: the significance of family, first in the foundation, and then the growth, of NASCAR.

The Frances—Bill Sr. and his wife Anne, along with sons Bill Jr. and Jim—set the standard: close-knit and hard-working, God-fearing but fun-loving, tough but fair. The Frances built NASCAR from the ground up, but they had plenty of help from other families.

The Flocks. The Pettys.

The Pearsons. The Earnhardts.

The Allisons, the Jarretts, and the Labontes.

The Wallaces and the Waltrips. And so many more.

But why are families so much more prevalent in NASCAR than other sports, particularly when racing is so much more dangerous than, say, baseball? Why is NASCAR so readily passed from one generation to the next?

Perhaps one reason is the sport's unique accessibility. While attributes needed to excel in *any* athletic endeavor—quickness, agility, keen reflexes—are vital for someone seeking to excel in racing, the atypical physical characteristics often required in, say, professional football or basketball, are by no means prerequisites for driving a stock car.

Also, it has been said that NASCAR is not merely a sport but a lifestyle, almost like growing up in a particular religion. If your father's into racing, there's a good chance *you're* going to be into racing. No way around it.

This book honors families who have truly lived the lifestyle, and who have contributed so greatly to the sport's success. Without these families, there may well be no NASCAR.

These names are now legend. More legends are in the making.

**ABOVE**: Richard and Lee Petty.
**BELOW**: Bob, Tim, and Fonty Flock.

# *The* FRANCE *Family*

LONG BEFORE THE CITY OF Daytona Beach, Florida, became the Birthplace of NASCAR, it was the Birthplace of Speed. Actually it was Ormond Beach, a few miles to the north, where the whole thing started, with turn-of-the-century competitions featuring daredevils from around the world, all chasing the world land-speed record on the hard-packed sands of the Atlantic Ocean shoreline.

When William Henry Getty France—Bill France Sr.—rolled into town on U.S. 1 in 1934, there was precedent already in place, in terms of both sport and ambition. Fast times and high rollers in the Daytona area dated to the late 1800s. The area had been home to Standard Oil magnate John D. Rockefeller for a while. An associate of Rockefeller's, developer extraordinaire Henry Flagler, rebuilt the magnificent Ormond Hotel, and in the process, brought his Florida coastal railroad expansion with him. Daytona Beach was for a short while the terminus of the Florida East Coast Railway that Flagler eventually took

OPPOSITE: Bill Sr. (center) in Pikeville, Maryland, 1931. ABOVE: Bill France Jr. in his father's race car, 1933.

all the way to Key West, fueling development along the state's east coast. It is hard to imagine what Florida would have been without Henry Flagler.

Yet it's easy to imagine that Flagler and Bill Sr. would've gotten on well. Both were irrepressible dreamers—and doers. Like Flagler, Bill's dreams were big, befitting his six-foot, five-inch height, and inevitable nickname "Big Bill."

Bill France Sr. started with little, but contrary to some accounts, he did not start with nothing. In many ways, he was already a rich man, long before the first turnstile spun at Daytona International Speedway. He had, after all, his family.

Bill France arrived with his wife, Anne, and year-old son, Bill Jr., having left their home near Washington, D.C. A mechanic by trade and a racer as a hobby, Bill Sr. took a job working on cars, and rented a small house a mile or so inland from the famous beach.

The next twenty-five years were eventful, to say the least.

# ENTRANTS

*v= 1.0*
*0: 65*

| CAR NO. | MAKE | DRIVER | ENTRANT | QUALIFYING SPEED |
|---|---|---|---|---|
| 14 | FORD | WALTER JOHNSON | O. L. MOODY | 63.92 |
| 5 | DODGE | WM. SCHINDLER | H. ATKINSON | 59.65 |
| 22 | FORD | "HICK" JENKINS | H. R. DIXON | 67.95 |
| 19 | FORD | SAM. PURVIS | SAM. PURVIS | 67.25 |
| 15 | FORD | DAN MURPHY | CARL PURSER | 63.96 |
| 17 | FORD | ED. ENG | DON SUTTLE | 64.28 |
| 29 | AUBURN | JOHN RUTHERFORD | JOHN RUTHERFORD | 65.97 |
| 16 | FORD | ALBERT CUSICK | ALBERT CUSICK | 64.25 |
| 9 | FORD | WM. LAWRENCE | WM. LAWRENCE | 62.81 |
| 11 | FORD | LOU CAMPBELL | L. S. CAMPBELL | 63.32 |
| 21 | FORD | BILL SOCKWELL | BILL SOCKWELL | |
| 3 | CHEVROLET | B. J. GIBSON | B. J. GIBSON | 61.47 |
| 1 | WILLYS 77 | LANGDON QUIMBY | LANGDON QUIMBY | 58.71 |
| 4 | WILLYS 77 | SAM COLLIER | SAM COLLIER | 58.60 |
| 24 | FORD | DOC. MACKINZIE | G. D. MACKENZIE | 67.92 |
| 18 | FORD | BEN SHAW | ED. PARKINSON | 66.01 |
| 6 | FORD | BOB SALL | RUDY ADAMS | 61.51 |
| 26 | FORD | TOMMY ELMORE | THOS. ELMORE, JR. | 62.3 |
| 20 | OLDSMOBILE 8 | KEN. SCHROEDER | FLOYD A. SMITH | 66.3 |
| 2 | AUBURN | BILL CUMMINGS | M. J. BOYLE | 70.3 |
| 25 | FORD | AL WHEATLEY | AL. WHEATLEY | 65.2 |
| 12 | FORD | AL PIERSON | AL. PIERSON | 63.5 |
| 27 | FORD | JACK HOLLY | JACK HOLLY | 68.0 |
| 28 | FORD | VIRGIL MATHIS | DAN H. STODDARD | 66.2 |
| 8 | FORD | GILBERT FARRELL | C. A. HARDY | 62.7 |
| 7 | LINCOLN ZEPHYR | MAJOR A. T. G. GARDNER | A. T. G. GARDNER | 61.7 |
| 10 | FORD | WILLIAM FRANCE | ISAAC BLAIR | 63.0 |
| 23 | FORD | MILTON MARION | MILT MARION | 66.1 |

## —FLAG SIGNALS—

| | |
|---|---|
| GREEN | Start of Race; Course is clear. |
| YELLOW | Caution; Bring car under control and reduce speed to 50 miles per hour. |
| ORANGE with BLUE CENTER | Competitor is attempting to overtake you |
| WHITE | Report at your pit on the next lap. |
| RED | Danger; stop. |
| BLUE | You are entering your last lap. |
| CHECKER | You have finished. |

**1936 NATIONAL CHAMPIONSHIP**
**BEACH AND ROAD RACE**
DAYTONA BEACH, FLORIDA

The first true step Bill Sr. took toward making auto racing his business came in 1936. The city of Daytona Beach, financially strapped in the middle of the Depression, was interested in reviving motorsports locally and, in the process, hoped to revive the city's economy. A former land-speed record holder named Sig Haugdahl, who had taken up residence in Daytona, was asked for guidance. Haugdahl had the idea to stage a race that would utilize a portion of the coastal highway, called A1A, as well as a stretch of the sandy beach.

France decided to enter the event, and along the way he became a partner of sorts with Haugdahl. The race lost a huge amount of money, but Bill Sr. was not dissuaded. He soon began promoting beach races himself, convinced of the potential of the concept.

Building the attractiveness of beach-road races was not an easy task. In addition, the process was halted for several years because of World War II. But not long after the war ended, interest in the sport accelerated, and Bill Sr. took the wheel.

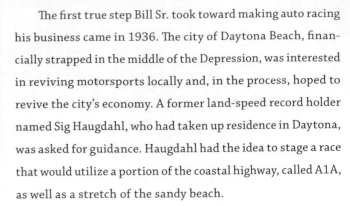

1938

THIS IS NOT A STAY IN PASS
AND
IS NOT GOOD FOR GATE ADMISSION

MR. *Bill France*

has permission to work in Garages
the night of May 29, 1938.

*J. W. G. Carpenter*
SAFETY DIRECTOR

**LEFT:** The 1936 Beach Race entrants list, including "William France." **ABOVE:** Bill Sr.'s 1938 garage work pass for the Indianapolis 500. **OPPOSITE:** Sig Haugdahl, 1936 Daytona course designer (right), with competitors Doc McKenzie (left) and Maj. Goldie Gardner.

| Mar 8 1936 | Milt Marion | '36 Ford Roadster | ✓ |
| | | | ✓ |
| | | | ✓ |
| March 1939 | John Rice | '39 Mercury | |
| July 4 1939 | Stewart Joyce | 32 Ford | |
| Saturday 1939 | Smoky Purser | 39 Mercury | ✓ |
| March 1940 | Roy Hall | .39 Ford | |
| July 7 1940 | Bill France | 39 century Buick | ✓ |
| Saturday 1940 | Cannon Ball Baker | 39 Ford | ✓ |
| March 1941 | Roy Hall | 39 Ford | ✓ |
| July 4 37 | | | |
| Saturday 37 | | | |
| July 4 38 | | | |
| Saturday 38 | | | |

**OPPOSITE:** Bill Sr. and Anne France at Daytona Beach in 1940.
**CLOCKWISE FROM BOTTOM LEFT:** Ad for Bill Sr.'s pre-NASCAR racing group; Bill Sr. leading the 1940 Beach Race; Bill Sr.'s handwritten Beach Race winner's list.

In 1946 and '47, he oversaw the National Championship Stock Car Circuit, the forerunner of NASCAR—only with "Modifieds," or cars that were heavily modified from stock form. Then, in December 1947, Bill Sr. gathered together a group of folks who were considered the leaders of the unorganized sport, with the goal of getting organized. The famed meeting, held from December 14 to 17 at the Streamline Hotel in Daytona Beach, resulted in the establishment of the National Association for Stock Car Racing—NASCAR.

Then came Strictly Stock—the revolutionary division created in 1949, and the grandfather of the NASCAR NEXTEL Cup Series. The Strictly Stock division evolved from Bill Sr.'s notion that people would buy tickets to see the same types of cars they drove on a daily basis.

Bill Sr., you see, had latched onto the elemental appeal of what would fuel NASCAR's growth, an appeal that separated stock cars from balls and bats, hoops and shoulder pads: a sense of identification with the sport. It's an appeal that still applies to this day: Not many people can dunk a basketball, while nearly everybody drives. And it's important to note that stock cars in the late 1940s really were, basically, the same machines being driven on the roads of America, minus some inevitable modifications. Many race cars in those days were actually driven to the race track—then driven back home, provided they were not too banged up.

In 1950, Darlington Raceway was born. A track that was shaped like an egg would help shape the future of NASCAR. Darlington's new event would be called the Southern 500, and it would quickly become one of NASCAR's major races.

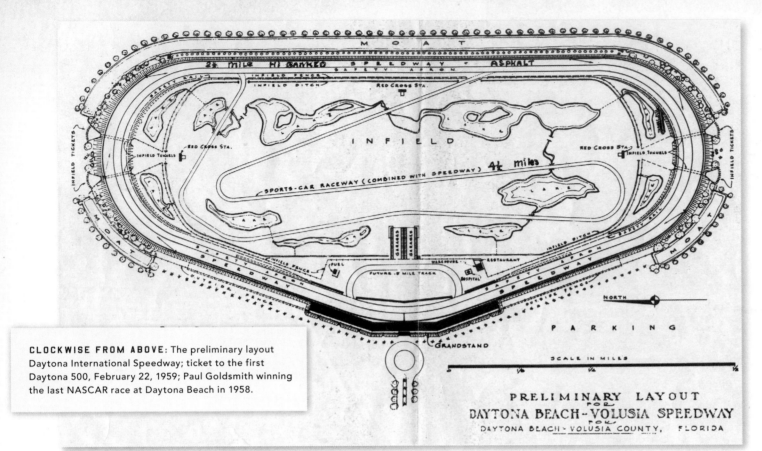

PRELIMINARY LAYOUT
FOR
DAYTONA BEACH–VOLUSIA SPEEDWAY
FOR
DAYTONA BEACH–VOLUSIA COUNTY, FLORIDA

**CLOCKWISE FROM ABOVE:** The preliminary layout Daytona International Speedway; ticket to the first Daytona 500, February 22, 1959; Paul Goldsmith winning the last NASCAR race at Daytona Beach in 1958.

## Memorabilia

**CLOCKWISE FROM TOP LEFT:** Bill France Sr.'s business card from the early 1940s. • Bill Sr.'s handwritten letter to a stockholder, on personal stationary, and three pages of a program from the Bill Sr. testimonial dinner in 1955, hosted by the City of Daytona Beach. • A 1959 sketch of a conceptual entrance to Daytona International Speedway.

The following year, Hudson Motor Car Company stepped up to the plate and became the first factory to support NASCAR efforts. Factory-backing was a staple of the NASCAR formula envisioned by Bill Sr.

From 1957 to '59, Bill Sr. and Bill Jr. led the way on construction of Daytona International Speedway, a 2.5-mile track that matched Indianapolis Motor Speedway in size. Finally, on February 22, 1959, the first Daytona 500 was held, won by Lee Petty in a photo finish over Johnny Beauchamp, a result requiring three days of examining photos to determine. Ever the promoter, Bill Sr. maximized the publicity value of the decision delay, helping to establish the Daytona 500 as the sport's most identifiable race.

The keys to NASCAR were passed on to Bill Jr. in the early seventies, and the transition was predictably smooth. "I know of some other father-son relationships that weren't very good, and the son couldn't do anything that the father approved of," Bill Jr. said. "I never had that problem. For us, it couldn't have been better from that standpoint." And about thirty years later, Bill Jr.'s son, Brian, would take NASCAR's wheel.

Since day one, this has been a family affair. From its humble beginnings to today's overwhelming popularity and economic windfall, NASCAR has been driven by the Frances, as leadership has passed through three generations of France men. And, always, the France women have played integral roles—whether running the organization's finances or contributing to its public relations, or, sometimes, making sure the husbands don't stray too far from their plans. As Lesa Kennedy, Bill Jr.'s daughter, recalls, "My grandfather was a visionary and my grandmother made sure it all stayed right on track."

They've stayed on "the right track" for three generations, and there's no reason to think that will change. The France family has accomplished something special indeed, and in the process has become the "First Family" of NASCAR.

# NASCAR *Newsletter*

VOL. XVII    JANUARY 15, 1972    No. 2

Petty Visits
Vietnam
See Page 5

## the president's corner

**Dear Member,**

This is the first time since the Newsletter was first published 17 years ago that Bill France did not appear as the president of NASCAR. From now on I'll be writing in this section of our official publication, and you can be sure that as time goes by, we'll be covering all forms of stock car racing and we'll also be speaking out on various issues.

As your new president, I'm confident that NASCAR will continue not only to lead other automobile racing sanctioning bodies but also will move forward rapidly in all facets of the sport of stock car racing. At 24 years of age NASCAR is still a young and growing organization and we have yet much to accomplish.

Bill France, Sr., since he founded NASCAR in 1947 and through the years has accomplished what I feel no other man could have done. When racing was a raw, unorganized maverick sport back in the '40s, he took it upon himself to work toward the day stock car racing would be recognized as one of the top professional sports in the country. I believe it is now. He saw the need for rules and order; he saw the importance of high safety standards; and he saw that drivers deserved insurance and hospitalization plans. In all these NASCAR has been first and will continue to be.

We all wish him in his retire-[ment] ... CAR much hap-[py] ... any enjoyable [re]commend him in [wha]t he has done

[I'd] like to add that [I look for]ward to working [with] operators, car [owne]rs in the future [for fi]ne people in [the fa]mily.

*France Jr.*

# Bill France Retires From Top Post, Bill France, Jr., Named New President

Bill France has announced his retirement as president of the National Association for Stock Car Auto Racing, effective immediately, and the promotion of William C. France, his son, to the top post of the sanctioning body.

France also stated that he will continue to be involved in NASCAR affairs in an advisory capacity and will continue as chairman of the board and president of the International Speedway Corporation which operates Daytona International Speedway and the Alabama International Motor Speedway at Talladega, Ala.

France, who is 62, said of his move, "In the past 24 years NASCAR has grown to be one of the largest and certainly the finest sanctioning body in the world. Bill, Jr., has lived with NASCAR all his life and has the foresight and capability to handle the varied and demanding duties of the position.

"We feel that the staff at NASCAR is of the highest quality, blending experienced personnel with young and talented people," he said, "I'm sure that NASCAR will continue its dynamic leadership in the sport of automobile racing."

France cited that his reasons for

**Bill France Announces Retirement**

**Bill, Jr., Takes Over Top Post**

retirement from NASCAR were to devote more time in the operations of the two superspeedways and to allow him added time [for] other endeavors.

France, Jr., on his new [post] stated, "Right now NASCAR [is] the largest stock car sanction[ing] body in the world. With the de[di]cation of our fine staff and leadership at NASCAR headquar[ters] and the cooperation of tr[ack] operators, car owners and driv[ers] I am sure that NASCAR will not only continue to grow but accelerate in its leadership in the sport [of] automobile racing."

In his long career in rac[ing] France has traveled from a m[e]chanic and a sometime race driv[er] to one of the most influential m[en] in international automobile rac[ing].

A native of Washington, D[.C.] France moved to Daytona Bea[ch] in 1934 and opened a service s[ta]tion. In the next couple years [he] competed in annual races on [the] beach, and in 1938 took over [as] promoter of the event. World W[ar] II postponed the races until 19[46] when France resumed the events.

He soon became aware that [the] fledgling sport of stock car rac[ing] needed some sort of organizati[on]. He became the driving force [for] such an action to set rules, encou[r]age larger purses, initiate a ho[s]pitalization plan for drivers a[nd]

(Continued on Page 4)

**LEFT:** Bill Jr. leading Bill Sr. at Talladega in 1969. **ABOVE:** The January 15, 1972, NASCAR newsletter announcing that Bill Jr. would replace the retiring Bill Sr.

NASCAR Royalty: (left to right) Amy, Bill Sr., Bill Jr., Anne, Lesa, J.C., Betty Jane, Brian, Sharon and Jennifer, and Jim, circa 1980. **OPPOSITE**: Bill Sr. playing with Jim (left) and Bill Jr., circa 1950.

## The FAMILY RECORDS

### William Henry Getty France
#### (SEPTEMBER 26, 1909-JUNE 7, 1992)

William was born in Washington, D.C., and known as Bill Sr. and "Big Bill." France was founder and first president of NASCAR, serving as president from 1948 to 1972.

### Anne Bledsoe France
#### (OCTOBER 29, 1904-JANUARY 2, 1992)

Anne, Bill Sr.'s wife, from Nathan's Creek, North Carolina, was known as "Annie B." She was responsible for managing the finances during NASCAR's formative years, serving as secretary-treasurer.

### William Clifton France
#### (APRIL 4, 1933-JUNE 4, 2007)

William, Bill Sr.'s son and known as Bill Jr., served as NASCAR's president from January 1971 until November 2000, when he was replaced by Mike Helton. Bill Jr. concurrently became chairman and CEO, presiding over NASCAR's newly formed board of directors. He stepped down in October 2003 to become vice chairman.

### Betty Jane France
#### (BORN APRIL 15, 1938)

Betty, Bill Jr.'s wife, is also NASCAR's assistant secretary. Betty Jane has become renowned for her work with charitable causes. She has been central to the establishment of racing-themed children's wards—called "Speediatrics"—at Halifax Medical Center in Daytona Beach, Florida, and Homestead (Florida) Hospital.

BELOW: Jim and Bill Sr. at Daytona Beach in 1956.
RIGHT: Bill Sr.'s recognition banquet in 1955.

### James Carl France
**(BORN OCTOBER 24, 1944)**

Jim, the younger brother of Bill Jr., is NASCAR's vice chairman and executive vice president, in addition to being vice chairman and CEO of the International Speedway Corporation.

### Brian Zachary France
**(BORN AUGUST 2, 1962)**

The son of Bill Jr. and Betty Jane, Brian served as vice president of NASCAR prior to becoming chairman and CEO in October 2003. He has been involved in a number of major deals and developments in recent years that have elevated NASCAR's popularity, including the establishment of the NASCAR Research and Development Center in Concord, North Carolina, and the securing of Sprint Nextel Communications as sponsor of NASCAR's top series—NASCAR NEXTEL Cup.

### Lesa France Kennedy
**(BORN MAY 24, 1961)**

Lesa, the daughter of Bill Jr. and Betty Jane, is vice president and assistant treasurer of NASCAR. She also is president of the International Speedway Corporation.

**TOP:** Betty Jane France, Anne France, and Lesa Kennedy. **BOTTOM:** Halifax Hospital board member David Sacks, Betty Jane France and former ISC executive Jim Foster at the opening ceremony for the Betty Jane France Pediatric Center.

ABOVE: Two newspaper articles announcing the approval of the Daytona International Speedway lease. RIGHT: Bill Sr. in what would become the tri-oval area of the Daytona track, 1958. OPPOSITE: Bill Jr. helping with Daytona International Speedway construction in 1958.

# The FAMILY STORIES

BILL FRANCE JR. ON A TRACTOR IS PERHAPS THE MOST FAMOUS photograph illustrating the difficult process of building Daytona International Speedway. It is a photo that captures a moment and, more importantly, a mindset. The Frances' resolve to complete the incredibly ambitious project was unshakable.

After getting the financial thumbs-up from his wife Anne, who diligently guarded NASCAR's money, Bill Sr. secured some investment partners to get the project under way. Once they started, they worked day and night, with a skeletal crew compared to modern construction projects.

The speedway was sculpted from approximately four hundred acres of dormant swampland, several miles to the west of the famed shoreline. It featured 31-degree banking in the turns and a unique tri-oval layout that gave the front

Ground breaking occurred in November 1957; the track opened for testing in January 1959. Ten years later, Bill Sr. built an even bigger, faster track, with even higher (33 degrees) banking, in Talladega, Alabama: the Talladega Superspeedway.

THE SHOT OF BILL FRANCE SR. HANDING a set of keys to a youthful Bill France Jr. in 1972 was a photo opportunity set up to symbolize a father handing over control of NASCAR to his son, who was assuming the role as NASCAR president. The photo also served as a metaphor for the changes that were sweeping across the sport in the early 1970s.

A year before, the R. J. Reynolds Tobacco Company had begun its sponsorship of NASCAR's premier series—and the NASCAR Winston Cup Series was born. The spin-off of this successful partnership—which lasted through the 2003 season—was that corporate America truly started noticing the viability of NASCAR as a means to market products to an incredibly loyal fan base, a fan base that also was showing loyalty to those companies that backed NASCAR.

Bill Sr. at the Daytona International Speedway groundbreaking in 1957.

stretch two "kinks," one coming out of Turn 4, the second going into Turn 1.

The idea for the severe banking angle was something Bill Sr. had become enamored with. He'd first seen the effect years before at Laurel (Maryland) Speedway, a mile-plus "board" oval—a track consisting of two-by-fours laid end-to-end and side-by-side, allowing for great speeds—and great racing.

But, perhaps more importantly, Bill Sr. wanted fans in the stands to *see* the racing. On a 2.5-mile track, banking would be the only way to achieve that goal.

So he landed on 31 degrees. If he could have made it steeper, he would have.

"That was high as we could stack the dirt without it rolling down the bank," Bill Jr. recalls.

Bill Jr. grabbed the keys and took off. Over the next thirty-one years, NASCAR's popularity would soar.

THERE WAS ANOTHER FATHER-SON HANDOFF IN OCTOBER 2003, WHEN Bill Jr. stepped down as chairman and CEO, and his son Brian stepped in—and immediately hinted that change was coming.

He wasn't kidding.

Brian's ascension came just two months after the announcement that Sprint Nextel would replace Winston as the title sponsor of NASCAR's premier series.

LEFT: Bill Sr. hands his son the NASCAR keys in 1972. BELOW: Brian France takes over the family business from his father in 2003.

That was big news, but within a year's time, that news had plenty of company.

The Chase for the NASCAR NEXTEL Cup was announced in early 2004, a dramatic departure from the traditional way of determining the premier series' champion. After twenty-six races, the top ten drivers in points (plus anyone else within four hundred points of the standings' leader) qualify for a ten-race shootout over the balance of the season. Brian said it would work, but skeptics abounded. The skeptics were wrong.

There was more innovation, such as talk of a race in the New York area—talk backed up when International Speedway Corporation (ISC) purchased a chunk of land on Staten Island.

NASCAR's expansion into Mexico was announced in 2004. Two NASCAR Busch Series events have been held in the past two years in Mexico City, at the famed road course with the lyrical name—Autodromo Hermanos Rodriguez.

Remember the epic network television contract signed prior to the 2001 season? It's been followed by a new contract taking effect in 2007, one heralded by the return of ABC and ESPN to the NASCAR fold, as they join returning partners FOX, FX, SPEED, and TNT.

"I'm not smart enough to look out fifteen or twenty years (like Bill Sr. and Bill Jr.)," Brian says. "But I do know what we have to do now—build a foundation to be successful in the long run. I'm bullish about that."

BILL FRANCE JR. HAS BEEN REPORTED TO BE ONE OF THE FIVE-HUNDRED richest men in the world. On the other hand, he's also renowned for frugality. In the old days, that translated into making a buck out of, well, sometimes nothing.

As a child, Bill Jr. sold sno-cones at a North Carolina short track. On one occasion, he ran out of syrup. No worries. He went on trying to sell them as plain sno-cones. Word is he actually sold some.

OPPOSITE: Bill Sr. welcomes Bill Jr. home from the Navy in 1956. ABOVE: Bill Jr. with his father in 1969.

Or those years when he had hot-dog making down to a fine, lucrative art at the old Charlotte–Southern States Fairgrounds. Bill ran the concession stand at the Fairgrounds track, an avenue that presented a few challenges. The track didn't have a kitchen, so upon arrival in Charlotte, a cheap hotel room was rented—one with a kitchenette. All hot dogs would be cooked in advance, instead of waiting to cook them until arriving at the track.

He would smother the dogs with canned chili, and throw a layer of Tabasco sauce on top. The plan was simple. "We used that Tabasco to sell more soft drinks,"

## Two-Day Program Starts At Noon

### Women's Race, Time Trials Set Stage For Running Of 150-Miler

Thousands of Daytona Beach's famous racing course will resound again today and tomorrow to the spinning wheels and roaring motors of speeding automobiles as a two-day program of stock car racing is staged on the road-beach course just south of the city.

Today's initial runnings will include a set of qualifying heats at noon—to enable drivers in tomorrow's 150-mile grind to be properly located in their pole positions—and the first women's stock car race ever to be staged here.

The main feature of the stock car program of course is the 150-mile marathon, set for 2 o'clock tomorrow afternoon, at which time a field of approximately 25 of the best drivers of the southeast will gun their mounts in quest of the title currently held by Bill France, veteran racing driver who won the July 7 running of the 150-miler.

But the women's race, which will get under way at 2:30 this afternoon, has come in for all of its share of attention, and probably will steal no little of the limelight usually reserved for the daredevils who will risk neck and fenders in tomorrow's running.

The girls' grind will be over a 25-mile distance — or eight laps of the 3.2 mile track — and promises to be one of the wildest exhibitions of daring driving that ever has been seen, on or off any race track in the country. Victory in the girls' race will be worth $50 to the winner — and watching the contest should be worth a dozen thrills a second for the spectators.

The spectators, incidentally, will be admitted to today's time trials and the women's race for a nominal admission price. Regular ad-

1—Mrs. Ethel Mobley of Atlanta.
2—Grace McLendon of Daytona Beach.
3—Maud Holland of Daytona Beach.
4—Mrs. Ann Crowe of Daytona Beach.
5—Evelyn Lee of Daytona Beach.
6—Mrs. Ruth Vogt of Atlanta.
7—Leona Szanto of Daytona Beach.
8—Mrs. Joe Littlejohn of Spartanburg, S. C.
9—Mrs. Ann France of Daytona Beach.
10—Mrs. Joe Brennan of Daytona Beach.

**ABOVE:** A *Daytona Beach News-Journal* article mentioning Anne France's participation in a women's race, Sept. 1, 1940. **RIGHT:** Bill Sr. and Anne France at Talladega, circa 1976. **OPPOSITE:** President Ronald Reagan meets Anne France on July 4, 1984.

Bill Jr. says, "because let me tell you, if you didn't want a soft drink when you came up to the concession stand, you sure did after taking a bite of that hot dog."

HAL MARCHMAN, A PASTOR IN THE DAYTONA BEACH AREA, CONDUCTED invocations for years at Daytona International Speedway. One time in the early 1960s, Hal couldn't make it because he was running late. Bill Sr. stepped in, of course. Since he founded the sport, built the speedway, and even raced back in the day, what was the big deal about an invocation?

Bill Sr. handled himself well. Then he got to the finish and made the decision to place a "personal stamp" on the prayer. Instead of closing with a simple "Amen," he instead offered this: "Sincerely yours, Bill France."

ANNE B. FRANCE'S INFLUENCE WAS IN THE BUSINESS END OF THINGS, as she always displayed a combination of acumen and instinct that invariably was on the mark, and crucial to the process of building NASCAR. "Listening to the fans is critical, and the moment you are not listening to your fans, you are closed; my grandmother taught everyone that," says Lesa France Kennedy.

But Anne did more than just keep the books when her husband was promoting

races on the beach-road course in Daytona Beach. On September 1, 1940, she raced herself, in an all-women's event. She finished in the latter half of the thirteen-driver field.

BETTY JANE FRANCE WAS BETTY Jane Zachary when she ventured to Daytona Beach in 1957, to enter the "Miss NASCAR" beauty contest. She was already Miss Winston-Salem (North Carolina), which was her hometown.

Although she didn't take home the true crown, a year later she was married to Bill France Jr.

"She didn't win the contest," Bill Jr. recalls, "but she won NASCAR."

WHAT IN THE WORLD WOULD BILL FRANCE SR. THINK OF TODAY'S NASCAR? Perhaps the person best qualified to answer is Bill France Jr., who recently was asked the same question.

"He would be amazed, but he would certainly be enjoying it, no doubt about that. He would like it, believe me. After all, he put a lot of hard work in it to get the thing started."

**ABOVE**: Betty Jane competes in the 1957 Miss NASCAR pageant. **OPPOSITE**: (left to right) Jim, Bill Sr., and Bill Jr., circa 1978.

# The JARRETTS

ERAS MESHED LATE IN THE afternoon of February 14, 1993, at Daytona International Speedway. The nation's NASCAR fans got to watch and listen and join in the emotional rollercoaster that made the last lap of the Daytona 500 even more special than usual, one of the most special in the long, grand history of NASCAR's greatest event.

Dale Jarrett was going to win the Daytona 500; he was going to win it for the first time, and win it to truly establish himself in the NASCAR NEXTEL Cup Series.

And more than anything, he was going to win it for his father.

Ned Jarrett used to rule this sort of racing. He was the series champion in 1961, and then again in '65. He won fifty races. Only nine drivers have won more. Ever.

OPPOSITE: Dale Jarrett (left) and owner Joe Gibbs get doused in a 1993 Daytona 500 victory celebration. ABOVE: Ned Jarrett wins at Darlington in 1965.

Because of the way he raced—clean and sportsmanlike, always—as well as his impeccable, professional demeanor off the track, Ned earned the nickname "Gentleman Ned." One thing they never called him, though, was Daytona 500 champion.

Ned Jarrett knew Daytona's frustration when Darrell Waltrip and Dale Earnhardt were in grade school. The guy was a pioneer in the art of winning the series championship but failing in the 500.

Unlike Waltrip and Earnhardt, Ned never broke through on NASCAR's biggest stage. Not that he wasn't close. The first time he ran the 500, in 1960, he finished sixth. His career-best 500 finish was third, in 1963—he ran out of gas while leading, with two laps to go. After that, there was a fifth-place run in '65, and a seventh in '66, his final shot.

Dale Jarrett taking the checkered flag at Daytona in 1993.

So on Valentine's Day of 1993, back at a place that had broken his heart many times, the Gentleman had another shot, albeit a vicarious one. His boy Dale was turning outlandish laps on the high banks while Ned watched from above— higher than the high banks even—from the press box, working as a color commentator for CBS.

In the closing laps, Dale Jarrett chased down that other Dale, who was trying to finally win the 500 in his fifteenth try. On the last lap, CBS producer Bob Stenner black-flagged protocol. He told play-by-play man Ken Squier to "lay out," TV-speak for get out of the way. Stenner had decided to let a father root his son home.

And so Ned did, his enthusiasm building by the second. As the two Dales raced out of Turn 4, the nation's viewers heard this: "Come on Dale! Go baby go! He's gonna make it . . . Dale Jarrett's gonna win the Daytona 500!"

He edged Earnhardt by less than a second.

Moments after Ned's call, CBS honed in on Martha Jarrett, Dale's mother, shedding tears of joy. Back to Ned in the booth. Somebody handed him a box of tissues. He needed them.

You want family? This was it, as real as it gets. And Ned Jarrett, by God, had a Daytona 500 victory that was sweeter than if he had won it himself. He said any of his NASCAR accomplishments paled compared to what Dale had done.

Dale, being interviewed by his dad on national TV, post-race, referenced the bad luck in '63.

"I got this one," Dale told his dad, "for you and all the family."

DAYTONA 500 BY STP POST-RACE

NED JARRETT (CBS TV Commentator, Dale Jarrett's father) -- (as CBS TV showed a picture of an emotional Martha Jarrett, Dale's mother, Ken Squier said 'Happy Valentine's Day, Mrs. Jarrett.') When Dale won his first race, at Michigan, in 1991, his mother wasn't there. I feel like running through the window (of the Winston Tower broadcast booth) and flying over there. He did exactly what he needed to do...(tongue in cheek) just like I told him to.

DALE JARRETT (#18 Interstate Batteries Chevrolet) -- I had just been trying to figure out where I could get a run on those guys. It seemed like three and four was a good place to get a run. I knew that I was kinda going to have to do it by myself. My car was really working good up high. I found out I could get on the outside of Jeff (Gordon) and I did that. Then, Dale (Earnhardt) just slipped up high down there (in turn three) -- it seemed like his car was a little loose getting into the corner, and I was still wide open and I was able to get in there on the bottom and get a run, and everything worked out perfect. We touched a little bit (entering the trioval) and I didn't know if I was going to be able to get by him. I think Geoff Bodine helped me get by him going into one. Once I got there, I thought they'd have a tough time getting by me. (Speaking to Ned Jarrett on CBS headset. "Super job, Dale! I'm really proud of you! You did just exactly what you had to do -- like I told you, right?" "That's right, dad. Exactly like you've told me all along. Thanks a lot for everything...this is a great day. You came so close, I believe, back in '63 when you ran out of fuel, I thought we'd get this one for the whole family." "Dale, your mother was praying for the last 15 laps," said Chris Economaki. "It was the longest prayer I ever heard anyone say.") Everything seemed to happen [...] the day. I had such a good car, I could just kinda bide [...] did a great job. We just want to thank the Lord for a [...] he one who brought this home for us. Rick Hendrick's [...] e got to thank him and Rick Wetzel (engine builder) -- [...] e that they gave me -- it just worked great all day [...] Jimmy Makar gave me a great race car -- what a way to [...]

[...] team owner #18 Interstate Batteries Chevrolet) -- This [...] I'm one of the most fortunate individuals in the world [...] L) Super Bowls and now, the Super Bowl of Motorsports.

[...] TT (Dale Jarrett's wife) -- I can certainly believe [...] ore we came down here, we were coming back from a [...] aid, in this real boyish fashion, 'I know I might be the [...] I feel like I might win the Daytona 500.'

BELOW: Transcript of Ned Jarrett's call of his son's Daytona victory. RIGHT: Post-race quotes from the 1993 Daytona 500.

TRANSCRIPT OF NED JARRETT CALL

COME ON DALE, GO BABY GO, ALRIGHT, COME ON...I KNOW HE'S GONE TO THE FLOORBOARD...HE CAN'T DO ANYMORE...COME ON, TAKE HER TO THE INSIDE, DON'T LET HIM GET ON THE INSIDE OF YOU COMIN' AROUND THE TURN...HERE HE COMES... EARNHART'S...IT'S DALE AND DALE AS THEY COME OFF TURN FOUR...YOU KNOW WHO I'M PULLING FOR AS DALE JARRETT...BRING HER TO THE INSIDE DALE, DON'T LET HIM GET DOWN THERE...HE'S GONNA MAKE IT, DALE JARRETT'S GONNA WIN THE DAYTONA 500 ALRIGHT!...LOOK AT MARTHA...OH CAN YOU BELIEVE IT!...

The Jarretts at the Daytona International Speedway in July 1961. OPPOSITE: (left to right) Martha, Patti, Glenn, Ned, and Dale Jarrett in 1965.

## Dale Jarrett
### (BORN NOVEMBER 26, 1956)

Dale, Ned's younger son, from Hickory, North Carolina, started the 2006 NASCAR NEXTEL Cup season with thirty-two victories, good for nineteenth on the all-time list. Included in that total are three Daytona 500 victories—1993, '96, and 2000.

He won the 1999 NASCAR NEXTEL Cup championship, and he has finished in the final standings' top five a total of seven times, a run that came in consecutive years, from 1996 to 2002.

He also was a "charter member" of the NASCAR Busch Series, racing in the series' inaugural season in 1982. He has eleven victories and fourteen poles in the series.

In 1998, he too was named one of NASCAR's 50 Greatest Drivers.

## The FAMILY RECORDS

## Ned Jarrett
### (BORN OCTOBER 12, 1932)

Ned was the champion of the NASCAR NEXTEL Cup Series in 1961 and '65. The Newton, South Carolina native won fifty races, which has him tied for tenth all-time with Junior Johnson. Forty-eight of his wins came on short tracks, the third-best short-track total all-time.

Little wonder he was named one of the NASCAR 50 Greatest Drivers in 1998.

## Glenn Jarrett
### (BORN AUGUST 11, 1950)

Glenn, Dale's older brother, raced sporadically in NASCAR national series competition from 1978 to '93. During those years he made ten NASCAR NEXTEL Cup starts, with his best finish coming in NASCAR's biggest race—the Daytona 500. In the 1981 500 he finished nineteenth, driving the Tuf-Lon of Florida Buick owned by Roger Hamby.

Glenn was also there for the first year of the NASCAR Busch Series, racing six events in 1982. Between 1982 and '93, he made sixty-seven NASCAR Busch Series starts, with thirteen top-ten finishes. His average finish was 19.4. His best finish was fourth, in the 1982 Miller Time 300, at Lowe's Motor Speedway in Concord, North Carolina.

## Jason Jarrett
### (BORN OCTOBER 14, 1975)

Jason, Dale's son, had forty-two NASCAR national series starts coming into 2006—two in NASCAR NEXTEL Cup. The other forty had come in the NASCAR Busch Series. Jason has been concentrating his efforts in the ARCA Series in recent years. His two NASCAR NEXTEL Cup starts came at Talladega in the fall of 2003 and Pocono in the summer of 2004. He posted finishes of twenty-ninth and fortieth, respectively.

In NASCAR Busch Series competition, his best finish prior to 2006 was sixteenth at Hickory, North Carolina. Jason's busiest NASCAR season came in 2002, when he raced seventeen times in Pontiacs and Chevrolets owned by Green Bay Packers quarterback Brett Favre, with sponsorship by Rayovac.

*Memorabilia*

Ned Jarrett's 1957 NASCAR information sheet. • A Jason Jarrett color postcard.

**LEFT:** Ned Jarrett, No. 11, out in front in 1963.
**OPPOSITE:** Ned Jarrett at Daytona in 1964.

THE YEAR WAS 1954. THE PLACE WAS THE OLD BEACH-ROAD COURSE in Daytona Beach, Florida. Sand racing aside, the seaside city was the stock car mecca even then, five years before the new Daytona International Speedway would open its gates for the first time.

February 20, the Modified-Sportsman race featured Ned Jarrett and 119 other drivers. Yes, a 120-car field.

Ned negotiated the high-speed traffic snarl in a Sportsman entry, a 1937 Ford. Things were moving along swimmingly, with Ned zipping north on the 4.1-mile circuit, the Atlantic Ocean to his right. Suddenly, the Ford was punted by a faster-moving Modified ride—right into the surf. Ned's Ford flipped into the water, eventually coming to rest upright.

A dazed Ned got out of his car and walked off the course before losing consciousness. He recalls waking up in the lap of an inebriated female fan who was trying to revive him the old-fashioned way—by pouring straight whiskey down his throat.

Being a devout Christian, Ned knew that even in his hazy state of mind,

there was no way he was getting liquored up. He has joked that if the "whiskey touched my lips I knew I'd never make it to heaven."

Ned said thanks but no thanks to the 80-proof, got up, and was transported to a local hospital for treatment of his injuries. He was sore—but sober.

NED JARRETT WON THE NASCAR NEXTEL CUP CHAMPIONSHIP IN 1961, even though he had only one victory and missed six races of the fifty-two-race schedule. You could do that in those days and get away with it, points-wise; everyone missed races here and there. Also, Ned made the most of the ones he did enter in '61, with twenty-three top fives and thirty-four top tens.

He followed up with better seasons statistically in 1962 and '63, but came up short in the title chase. In retrospect, those two seasons, when he won a total of fourteen events, set Ned up for one of the best back-to-back efforts in NASCAR history.

In 1964 and '65, Ned ran a total of 113 events, missing only four on the schedule. Fifteen victories in '64, thirteen more in '65, forty-five top tens each

year—and his second series championship, in '65. The highlight of that championship run had to be winning the Southern 500 by an incredible fourteen laps—that comes out to 17.5 miles on a 1.366-mile track—which still stands as the largest margin of victory in NASCAR history.

Granted, his second title was aided by Chrysler's boycott of NASCAR that season, after the manufacturer's new 426 Hemi engine was disallowed. Ford was left to dominate, and Ned was Ford's lead driver. What went around came around, though. During the 1966 campaign, Ford announced a reduction in their NASCAR effort after new rules allowed the Chrysler engine on some short tracks. Coincidentally, Ned had already been contemplating a reduction of his NASCAR effort.

The season finale at Rockingham proved to be Ned's finale as well. "My children were growing up and I wanted to spend more time with the family," Ned recalls.

For a while, he promoted races at Hickory Speedway. Eventually, his affable demeanor and inherent knowledge of racing led him to another niche job—that of a racing broadcaster, first on radio, then on television.

Over the years, Ned has voiced some regrets over leaving the sport at the age of thirty-four. "I set certain goals for myself and vowed that however far up the ladder I was, I'd quit when I was there and not go down the other side, and I managed to reach those goals. We thought like other athletes, you get to your mid-thirties and you start losing your ability and competitive edge, but we've learned that race drivers can go much longer than that and continue to get more effective as time goes by. There have been times that I regretted it."

# Jarrett Captures Darlington As Leaders Fail

9/7/65

DARLINGTON, S.C. (AP) — Ned Jarrett won the Southern 500 stock car race Monday after mechanical troubles sidelined the day's two top leaders, Darel Dieringer and Fred Lorenzen, with 41 laps to go.

**Auto Racing**

Jarrett, 32-year-old factory Ford driver from Camden, S.C., collected the $20,200 first prize money and will also earn some money for the 63 laps he led the race.

Buddy Baker, driving the 1965 Plymouth started in the race by his father, three-time winner Buck Baker, finished second.

Dieringer finished third, although he drove from the 323rd lap without brakes; Buddy Arrington finished fourth, and Roy Mayne in a 19__ Chevrolet was fifth.

Jarrett, known as the gentlem__

of the stock car crowd and one of the best short track drivers around, put his Ford in the lead for good on the 326th lap over the 1 3/8 mile Darlington International Raceway and sailed home without any serious challenge.

The Bakers took home $9,100.

Dieringer, whose day was surely the most frustrating of his 10-year career, led for 187 laps of the 364 turns on this demanding highly-banked oval, and appeared to be safely home with his only victory of the year when his brakes failed on his aging 1964 Mercury.

Arrington drove a Dodge.

A number of caution flags held the average down to 115.878 miles per

★　★　★　★

• 43 •

WHEN DALE JARRETT BECAME A FULL-TIME DRIVER IN THE NASCAR NEXTEL Cup Series in 1987, it was clear that he, too, was a gentleman, with a personality pulled from his father's playbook. One thing that was not clear, however, was where his career would lead, in terms of accomplishments.

It is worth noting that Dale Jarrett wasn't nessarily a born race-car driver. He was a fine high school athlete with scholarship ability, mainly in golf. After graduation from high school, though, racing's allure won out over college. Dale followed his destiny on a path established by his father.

Prior to 1987, Dale had shown potential, but it wasn't what many considered *championship* potential. Five years in the NASCAR Busch Series, from 1982 to '86, produced one victory. Four appearances in NASCAR NEXTEL Cup (three in '84, one in '86) were nondescript. Then came his first four seasons at NASCAR's top rung—winless, all.

Slowly, though, things started to change. Dale got his first NASCAR NEXTEL Cup victory at Michigan in 1991, snapping a 134-race winless streak for his car owners, the Wood Brothers. In '92, he was the first driver for a new team that carried a distinct novelty quality, as it was owned by Joe Gibbs, the man who coached

OPPOSITE ABOVE: Dale (center) with his first Late Model car. Future crew chief Andy Petree is at left, circa 1980. OPPOSITE BELOW: Glenn Jarrett, No. 24, leads a NASCAR Busch Series race in 1983. ABOVE: Dale Jarrett, No. 18, leads the 1987 Daytona 500. LEFT: Dale in 1991, driving for the Wood Brothers.

LEFT: Dale's first NASCAR NEXTEL Cup win, at Michigan in 1991. BELOW: Dale in front of his Daytona-winning car.

the Washington Redskins to three Super Bowl championships. In '93, Dale's second series victory was also his first Daytona 500 win, a season-opening upset that pointed him in the right direction; he finished fourth in the final points.

In '95, Dale joined Robert Yates Racing, driving the famed No. 28 Ford, replacing Ernie Irvan, who had been severely injured the previous year in an accident. A year later, he moved over full-time to the No. 88 Ford, and a partnership with crew chief Todd Parrott, and his potential became realized.

He opened '96 by winning the Daytona 500 again, and went on to finish third in points. In '97, he won a career-high seven races, and finished second in the standings. In '98, he again finished third in the points.

So, unlike that first Daytona 500 victory, Dale's run to the series championship in 1999 surprised no one. His four victories included a second Brickyard 400 triumph, and were complemented by unmatched consistency: he led the series in both top fives (twenty-four) and top tens (twenty-nine).

Dale finally had his title, and in the process, had earned it with the dignity and grace his father had displayed so many years before.

Ned (second from right) and Dale Jarrett in Victory Lane at the 1996 Brickyard 400 in Indianapolis.

**ABOVE**: Glenn Jarrett covering a race. **OPPOSITE**: Glenn interviews Rusty Wallace.

GLENN JARRETT SPENT MOST OF HIS RACING CAREER IN THE NASCAR Busch Series. After he was done racing in 1993, Glenn followed his father's lead again, also becoming a broadcaster, primarily in radio, as one of the best pit reporters in the industry. These days, Glenn is the CEO and vice president of the Dale Jarrett Racing Adventure organization, based in Newton, North Carolina. DJRA, begun in 1998, offers entertainment-based oval driving schools and events, with both riding and driving programs at various levels of expertise.

Early in 2006, Jason Jarrett joined the organization. As always, whether on or off the track, the Jarrett family remains united.

# *The* FLOCKS

A MAN AND HIS MONKEY.

That is the inescapable one-liner history has left us regarding the NASCAR exploits of the Flock family from Fort Payne, Alabama, a small town tucked into the north-eastern corner of a state that was considered the heart of NASCAR country in the 1950s.

That line evokes an entertaining image whenever the Flocks are mentioned, but also obscures the remarkable achievements of four racing siblings, including one pioneering female, who collectively helped NASCAR build its foundation.

Blame this on the monkey.

Suffice it to say, NASCAR was different in those days. Today there are in-car cameras. There was a time when there were in-car monkeys.

As a public relations gimmick, a Rhesus monkey named "Jocko Flocko"

OPPOSITE: Tim, Ethel, and Fonty Flock in 1950. ABOVE: Fonty, Bob, and Tim Flock in Martinsville, Virginia, in 1955.

rode shotgun for a portion of the 1953 season alongside the most accomplished of the four Flocks, two-time NASCAR NEXTEL Cup Series champion Tim Flock.

Tim's older brothers were Bob and Fonty. Their sister was Ethel. The fact that all four raced can doubtless be traced to daredevil lineage. Their father Carl earned a living, in part, as a tightrope walker. That followed a brief career as a bicycle racer. There's more: their sister Reo was a "wing-walker" in an air show, with her husband flying a biplane. Brother Carl Jr. raced speedboats.

High wires, monkeys, and wing-walking conjure up circus thoughts. Again, because of that, there is a chance of minimizing these capable competitors. Time out, then, for a visit to the records, and a rundown of each fantastic Flock's on-track results—Jocko excluded.

**CLOCKWISE FROM LOWER LEFT:** Tim Flock and his 300SL Mercedes Benz; the Flock boys and their wives: (left to right) Ruby, Frances, Margie, and Punkin, with mother Maude Flock (center); Bob and Fonty Flock in 1953.

## Bob Flock

### (APRIL 16, 1918–MAY 16, 1964)

Bob Flock's career was ended prematurely by injuries sustained in a racing accident, but his relatively brief time on the circuit—seven years and thirty-six starts—added to the family legacy considerably.

Bob won four races in what is now known as the NASCAR NEXTEL Cup Series. He also had eleven top fives, eighteen top tens, and two poles.

In the very first season for what would become NASCAR NEXTEL Cup, Bob competed in six of eight races, and won two of them. He ended up third in the final point standings.

After a peek at his statistics compiled during NASCAR's early years, it's easy to envision a "what-might-have-been" scenario in which he would have rivaled the efforts of brothers Tim and Fonty.

## Ethel Flock

### (MARCH 8, 1920–JUNE 26, 1984)

Ethel, an accomplished Modified competitor, ran only two NASCAR NEXTEL Cup events, both in 1949. One of those events has become part of NASCAR lore: July 10 on the famous Daytona Beach, Florida, beach-road course, which utilized the hard-packed sands of the Atlantic Ocean shoreline and a por-

tion of State Road A1A. All four Flock siblings were in the same event that day. Tim finished second to Red Byron. Fonty was nineteenth, and Bob was twenty-second—both behind Ethel, who ran eleventh.

Ethel also ran at Langhorne (Pennsylvania) Speedway that season, finishing forty-fourth, which was next-to-last. At least she finished ahead of Fonty, who was, alas, last.

## Fonty Flock

### (MARCH 21, 1921–JULY 15, 1972)

Fonty had a stellar career that produced nineteen NASCAR NEXTEL Cup victories, seventy-two top tens, eighty-three top fives and thirty-three poles. An obvious highlight: winning the Southern 500 in 1952, while driving an Oldsmobile "Rocket 88" owned by Frank Christian.

In 1951, Fonty had a series-high eight wins and finished second in the final point standings—146.20 behind champion Herb Thomas and 339.75 ahead of his brother, future two-time titlist Tim Flock.

In 1947, Fonty was the best, winning the championship of the NCSCC—the National Championship Stock Car Circuit, the prototype for NASCAR and also run by Bill France Sr.

## Tim Flock

### (MAY 11, 1924–MARCH 31, 1998)

The NASCAR NEXTEL Cup Series champion in 1952 and '55, Tim Flock won thirty-nine races in only 189 starts between 1949 and '61—a winning percentage of .212 that still stands as the series' record. His victory total is fifteenth on the all-time list, ahead of outstanding drivers like Dale Jarrett, Fred Lorenzen, and Mark Martin.

In 1955, he won NASCAR's only sports car race, driving a Mercedes-Benz 300SL in a "one-off" deal held in that sports car capital of the world, Raleigh, North Carolina.

But more importantly, in 1955 he enjoyed one of the greatest seasons in the history of NASCAR, driving Chrysler 300s for legendary car owner Carl Kiekhaefer. Tim dominated: In forty-one starts he had eighteen victories, thirty-two top-five finishes, and nineteen poles. At the end of his career he had compiled an average finish of 9.5.

Tim died in 1998, at the age of seventy-three. A month earlier, in Daytona Beach during Speedweeks, Tim was named one of NASCAR's 50 Greatest Drivers, an appropriate tribute.

Ethel Flock poses with her car in 1948.

WHAT'S IN A NAME? THERE was, incidentally, a flock of Flocks raised by Lee and his wife Maudie. In addition to Tim, Fonty, Bob, and Ethel, there were four other siblings—Reo, Irene, Jackie, and Carl.

Of the lot, Reo had the most interesting name and the most interesting story behind it. She was named after the car company founded by the man who also founded Oldsmobile—Ransom Eli Olds, hence the R.E.O.

After a dispute with investors, Olds left Oldsmobile in 1904 and founded R.E.O. Soon, the new company was outselling the old.

Reo, incidentally, was given the middle name of Cleo.

As for Ethel, her name doesn't have quite as romantic an origin—unless you're a mechanic, whereupon you probably think it's quite romantic indeed. Ethel was named after, well, *ethyl,* which once was the commonly used name for commercial leaded gasoline. The name comes from the Ethyl Corporation, which made the "anti-knock" component, tetraethyl lead.

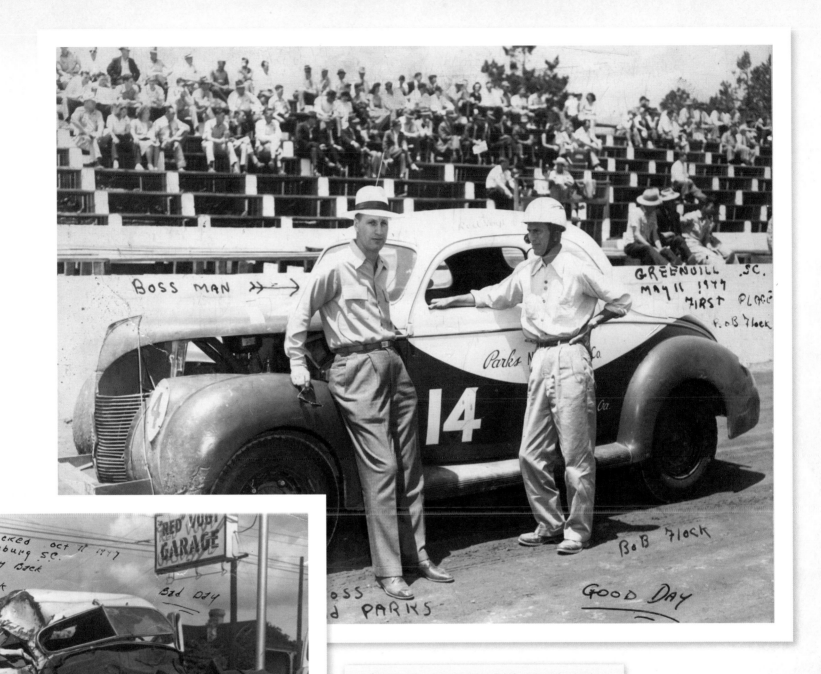

LEFT: An October 1947 crash left Bob with a broken back as he noted on the picture. ABOVE: Bob Flock (right) after winning in Greenville, South Carolina, in May 1947 with Raymond Parks.

*Memorabilia*

CLOCKWISE FROM TOP LEFT:
Pages one and two of Tim
Flock's NASCAR information
sheet from 1956. • Tim's handwritten monkey tale. • A 1948
NASCAR race report detailing
the Flock brothers finishing
first, second, and fourth.

## Jocko Flocko
## Stock Car Co-pilot
## 1953

| Date | Site | Finish | Winnings |
|---|---|---|---|
| 4/5/53 | Charlotte | 4 | $ 350 |
| 4/19/53 | Richmond | DNS | 0 |
| 4/26/53 | Macon | 6 | 150 |
| 5/3/53 | Langhorne | 5 | 500 |
| 5/9/53 | Columbia, SC | 2 | 700 |
| 5/16/53 | Hickory | 1 | 1,000 |
| 5/17/53 | Martinsville | 32 | 20 |
| 5/24/53 | Columbus, OH | 22 | 25 |
| 5/30/53 | Raleigh | 3 | 1,200 |
| | | | $3,945 |

OPPOSITE: Tim and Jocko, with the monkey's "driving" record. ABOVE: Tim and Fonty Flock go head-to-head in Dayton, Ohio, in 1951.

IN CASE YOU'RE WONDERING JUST HOW TIM FLOCK'S "MONKEY business" came about, it's first worth knowing that he wasn't alone in this 1950s tomfoolery that was aimed at adding to the entertainment experience. Frankie Schneider, a legendary Northeastern driver, also raced with a Rhesus from time to time.

In the 1950s, NASCAR was fighting for every bit of attention it could get. Racing was entertainment. The occasional dose of gimmickry was acceptable, if it helped turn the turnstiles.

The Rhesus monkey who would come to be known as Jocko Flocko was "discovered" in 1953 by Tim Flock's car owner at the time, Ted Chester. Chester envisioned a public relations boost. Flock envisioned, well, something. He just wasn't sure what.

Without consulting NASCAR, Jocko was installed as the "copilot." He was even outfitted accordingly, with his own driving suit. Fans, especially children, loved him.

The partnership, however, lasted all of eight races.

In those days, drivers checked right-front tire wear by pulling a chain that pulled up a flap sitting above the tire. A driver could literally monitor tire wear while racing. The story goes that Jocko scampered down to the flap and, when it was opened, he was nailed in the eye by race-track debris. The monkey went wild, jumping all over the race car, eventually landing on Tim's back. That forced a most unique type of pit stop, and Jocko was removed—permanently. The pitting had caused Tim to lose precious ground and, in the end, precious prize money.

THE JULY 10, 1949, DAYTONA BEACH RACE CAN BE SEEN IN retrospect as the ancestor of the Firecracker 400 and Pepsi 400. It was the second-ever "Strictly Stock" division event, which was also an ancestor of today's NASCAR NEXTEL Cup Series.

Obviously, a historically significant event for those reasons. With time, the four-Flock factor has added to the significance, as it was one of only two times in NASCAR's premier series that all four Flock siblings competed together.

Ethel—whose legal name was Ethel Flock Mobley, as she was married to car owner Charley Mobley—was part of a group of ardent female NASCAR racers who laid part of the foundation for today's full-speed diversity intiatives. Ethel Flock, Sara Christian, and Louise Smith all ran during the 1949 season.

THE INAUGURAL STRICTLY STOCK EVENT, HELD JUNE 19, 1949, at the three-quarter-mile dirt track at Charlotte Speedway, was full of Flock flavor. All three brothers were entered.

Bob took the pole, but his Hudson's engine blew, relegating him to thirty-second. Fonty finished second to Jim Roper, also driving a Hudson. Tim, who started second—making it a Flock front row—finished fifth in an Oldsmobile.

On the Flock brothers racing together, Frances Flock, widow of Tim Flock, says, "All three of them would rather outrun their brothers than anybody else

## A Flock Of Flocks

THE Flock brothers are just one, big happy family—until the starter's flag drops. Then they go after each other, wide open. Fontello Flock (left), 27 year old driver, won the national stock car title in 1947 and he was runnerup last year; Tim Flock (center), 23, is a rising young star; and Bob Flock (right), 31, is another topline veteran who has won in Daytona Beach twice. They are entered in the Sunday 200-mile national championship beach-road race here; and the Atlanta brothers will be driving cars built by rival mechanics. No holds are barred, once the starter's flag drops.

**CLOCKWISE FROM LOWER LEFT:** Tim (far left) and Bob Flock start in the front row of the first NASCAR NEXTEL Cup Series race in June 1949; Fonty (left) and Bob battle in 1948; A newspaper clipping about (left to right) Fonty, Tim, and Bob Flock.

# NASCAR BULLETIN

Dear Member:

Every day we get mail from the press and magazines, requesting information on drivers and other NASCAR members. To be able to answer these requests properly, we're planning to build up a complete file here at NASCAR headquarters so we'll have all this information at our fingertips. A little publicity has never hurt any driver as you'll agree. Please cooperate by filling out the following form and returning it pronto to our new home here at 42 South Peninsula Drive. If you have a picture of yourself, we'd like to have it, too, for our files. We prefer a picture about two by three, but any will be fine.

### NASCAR PRESS QUESTIONNAIRE

Name _FONTELL_ _FLOCK_ Nickname _FONTY_
First Middle Last

Address _____ Garage Ft. Payne, City State
Street _Ala._ 1921 How many years in racing? _11 YEARS_
Birthdate _MARCH 21_

Occupation (if other than racing) _SALESMAN_
Education: High School? _TECH HIGH_ Where? _ATLANTA_
College? _6 months_ Where? _ARMY_

Married? _YES_ Children _1 BOY 10 YRS 2 GIRLS 3 & 17 months_
Favorite drink _MILK_ Favorite food _STEAKS_
Did you ever take part in other sports? _FOOTBALL (HIGH SCHOOL)_

What are your hobbies besides racing? _ART_

What has been your biggest thrill or thrills in racing? _BEING RECOGNIZED AT_
_INDIANAPOLIS by most of ALL the drivers._ _PICTURE on the front of SPEED AGE._
_CARS to the NORTH TURN this year AT DA_
What would be your advice to beginners in auto racing? _S_
_CAR thats NOT too hot. ASK ADVICE of_
_FRANCE, SALL, etc. KEEP your mind on Y_
_RACE DON'T GET OVER ANXIOUS AND DR_
What NASCAR division or divisions do you race in? _GRAN_
When was your first race? _Lakewood-1938_ Favorite type
How did you make out in first race? _TURNED OVER_
How did you get started in racing? _RACED IN FIRST_

What tracks have you raced? _TRAVELED MORE THAN_
_1951 MAKING ALL RACES - MORE THAN_
Approximately how many races have you competed in? _3_
Ever injured? _YES_ When? _1940 - 1941_ WH

Who do you consider best driver? _TIM FLOCK_ B
Favorite car for racing _OLDS_

If you have any other information you think might be in please write below or the other side of the sheet if ne above spaces aren't enough, you're welcome to write as other side, too.)
_I TRAVELED 19,000 MILES_
NASCAR PB Form 1 _RACES IN CALI., N. CAROLINA, A_
_GRAND NATIONAL RACE this_
_That is, if there wasn't_

on the race track. If Fonty was leading and Tim could pass him, he'd blow him off the track. No matter which one it was, they absolutely got thrilled passing the other one, and taking the spot away from him. Tim used to say brotherly love leaves when you're on the race track."

TWENTY-EIGHT TIMES, THE THREE FLOCK BROTHERS APPEARED IN the same race. It seems appropriate that of the twenty-eight times the three Flock brothers raced together in NASCAR's top series, the brother with the two series championships ended up with the best bro-to-bro result. Fourteen times in this tri-sibling rivalry, Tim was the highest-finishing Flock. Fonty earned that honor eight times, while Bob did so six times.

   That said, it's worth noting that Tim Flock maintained throughout his life that Bob was the best driver of the three.

# The LABONTES

OPPOSITE: Bobby and Terry Labonte in Phoenix, Arizona, 1994, at the SLICK 50 500. ABOVE: Bobby, Bob Sr., and Terry Labonte, 1991.

THERE HAVE BEEN TWENTY-seven champions of NASCAR's premier series, now known as the NASCAR NEXTEL Cup Series, dating back to the inaugural season in 1949 and running through 2005. Two families have had fathers win championships and then be followed by their sons: the Pettys (Lee and Richard) and the Jarretts (Ned and Dale). Terry and Bobby Labonte share a different distinction, as the only brothers to win the NASCAR NEXTEL Cup title. Terry, the eldest, captured crowns in 1984 and '96; Bobby followed up with the 2000 title.

The Labontes also share another distinction, as the only drivers from the state of Texas to win the championship. That's somewhat surprising, considering that there have been fifty-one Texas natives who have driven in NASCAR's premier series since 1949. This was a list before its time, one that long ago shouted to the nation that NASCAR was not a Southeastern-only sport, as the well-worn stereotype—that still exists to this day, somewhat—would have you believe.

None of these Texans, however, can measure up to the NASCAR NEXTEL Cup exploits of the Labonte brothers, who hail from Corpus Christi. Raised to be racers by their father, Bob Sr.—who was crew chief for Bobby in the NASCAR

**NASCAR Winston Cup Series**

NASCAR WINSTON CUP RACE NO. 11
COCA-COLA 600 - CHARLOTTE MOTOR SPEEDWAY
Charlotte, NC - May 28, 1995
1.5 Mile High Banked Paved Speedway
600 M - 400 L - Purse: $1,484,184

| Fin Pos | Str Pos | Car No | Driver | Team | Laps | NASCAR Winston Cup Points | Bonus Points | Total Money Won | Reason Out Of Race |
|---|---|---|---|---|---|---|---|---|---|
| 1 | 2 | 18 | Bobby Labonte | Interstate Batteries Chevrolet | 400 | 180 | * 5 | $163,850 | Running |
| 2 | 13 | 5 | Terry Labonte | Kellogg's Chevrolet | 400 | 175 | * 5 | 93,050 | Running |
| 3 | 5 | 30 | Michael Waltrip | Pennzoil Pontiac | 400 | 170 | * 5 | 70,650 | Running |
| 4 | 7 | 4 | Sterling Marlin | Kodak Film Chevrolet | 399 | 165 | * 5 | 62,700 | Running |
| 5 | 18 | 10 | Ricky Rudd | Tide Ford | 399 | 160 | * 5 | 49,000 | Running |
| 6 | 34 | 3 | Dale Earnhardt | GM Goodwrench Service Chevrolet | 399 | 155 | * 5 | 52,500 | Running |
| 7 | 12 | 26 | Hut Stricklin | Quaker State Ford | 399 | 146 | | 30,000 | Running |
| 8 | 16 | 9 | Lake Speed | Spam/Melling Ford | 398 | 142 | | 27,500 | Running |
| 9 | 23 | 43 | Bobby Hamilton | STP Pontiac | 398 | 138 | | 25,400 | Running |
| 10 | 3 | 41 # | Ricky Craven | Kodiak Chevrolet | 397 | 134 | | 30,400 | Running |
| 11 | 10 | 21 | Morgan Shepherd | Citgo Ford | 397 | 135 | * 5 | 28,300 | Running |
| 12 | 29 | 90 | Mike Wallace | Heilig-Meyers Ford | 397 | 127 | | 20,800 | Running |
| 13 | 39 | 29 | Steve Grissom | Meineke Chevrolet | 397 | 124 | | 21,500 | Running |
| 14 | 15 | 1 | Rick Mast | Skoal Racing Ford | 397 | 121 | | 23,300 | Running |
| 15 | 27 | 16 | Ted Musgrave | The Family Channel Ford | 397 | 118 | | 23,300 | Running |
| 16 | 11 | 15 | Dick Trickle | Ford Quality Care Ford | 397 | 115 | | 20,550 | Running |
| 17 | 36 | 37 | John Andretti | Kmart/Little Caesars Ford | 396 | 112 | | 14,600 | Running |
| 18 | 21 | 17 | Darrell Waltrip | Western Auto Chevrolet | 396 | 109 | | 18,750 | Running |
| 19 | 26 | 12 | Derrike Cope | Straight Arrow Ford | 396 | 106 | | 13,000 | Running |
| 20 | 9 | 87 | Joe Nemechek | Burger King Chevrolet | 395 | 103 | | 11,350 | Running |
| 21 | 33 | 32 | Chuck Bown | Fina/Lance Chevrolet | 394 | 100 | | 8,800 | Running |
| 22 | 42 | 98 | Jeremy Mayfield | RCA Ford | 394 | 97 | | 11,650 | Running |
| 23 | 41 | 22 # | Randy LaJoie | MBNA America Pontiac | 393 | 94 | | 16,725 | Running |
| 24 | 25 | 33 # | Robert Pressley | Skoal Bandit Chevrolet | 393 | 91 | | 15,820 | Running |
| 25 | 8 | 27 | Elton Sawyer | Hooters Ford | 392 | 88 | | 16,300 | Running |
| 26 | 28 | 7 | Geoff Bodine | Exide Batteries Ford | 391 | 85 | | 22,000 | Running |
| 27 | 38 | 23 | Jimmy Spencer | Camel Cigarettes Ford | 390 | 82 | | 10,250 | Engine |
| 28 | 32 | 6 | Mark Martin | Valvoline Ford | 390 | 84 | * 5 | 21,310 | Running |
| 29 | 40 | 42 | Kyle Petty | Coors Light Pontiac | 380 | 76 | | 14,480 | Running |
| 30 | 6 | 25 | Ken Schrader | Budweiser Chevrolet | 358 | 83 | * 10 | 40,300 | Engine |
| 31 | 37 | 81 | Kenny Wallace | TIC Financial Systems Ford | 333 | 70 | | 6,750 | Rear End |
| 32 | 22 | 28 | Dale Jarrett | Texaco Havoline Ford | 317 | 67 | | 21,050 | Engine |
| 33 | 1 | 24 | Jeff Gordon | DuPont Refinishes Chevrolet | 283 | 69 | * 5 | 64,950 | Suspension |
| 34 | 24 | 2 | Rusty Wallace | Miller Genuine Draft Ford | 258 | 66 | * 5 | 22,500 | Handling |
| 35 | 4 | 11 | Brett Bodine | Lowe's Ford | 230 | 58 | | 21,950 | Accident |
| 36 | 31 | 19 | Loy Allen | Healthsource Ford | 225 | 55 | | 6,405 | Accident |
| 37 | 35 | 71 | Dave Marcis | Olive Garden Chevrolet | 159 | 52 | | 6,360 | Engine |
| 38 | 14 | 75 | Todd Bodine | Factory Stores Ford | 146 | 54 | * 5 | 11,920 | Engine |
| 39 | 19 | 94 | Bill Elliott | McDonald's Ford | 134 | 46 | | 6,320 | Accident |
| 40 | 20 | 8 | Jeff Burton | Raybestos Ford | 134 | 43 | | 11,320 | Camshaft |
| 41 | 30 | 31 | Ward Burton | Hardee's Chevrolet | 71 | 40 | | 6,320 | Accident |
| 42 | 17 | 97 | Chad Little | Harris Teeter Ford | 9 | 37 | | 6,320 | Engine |

# Maxx Race Cards Rookie of the Year Contender.   * Includes race leader/most laps bonus.

TIME OF RACE: 3 hours, 56 minutes, 55 seconds   AVERAGE SPEED: 151.952 mph TRACK RECORD   MARGIN OF VICTORY: 6.28 seconds
BUSCH POLE AWARD: Jeff Gordon, DuPont Refinishes Chevrolet (183.861 mph, 29.370 seconds)
BUSCH BEER FASTEST SECOND-ROUND QUALIFIER: Greg Sacks, Kendall Pontiac
AP PARTS MEET THE CHALLENGE AWARD: Steve Grissom, Meineke Chevrolet (26 positions improved)
TRUE VALUE HARD CHARGER AWARD: Ken Schrader, Budweiser Chevrolet (B. Labonte, Earnhardt)
GATORADE FRONT RUNNER AWARD: Ken Schrader, Budweiser Chevrolet
RCA PIT STRATEGY AWARD: Doug Hewitt, Pennzoil Pontiac
PLASTI-KOTE WINNING FINISH AWARD: Jimmy Makar, Interstate Batteries Chevrolet
TEAMWORK OF EXCELLENCE AWARD FROM UAW-GM: Jimmy Makar, Interstate Batteries Chevrolet
WESTERN AUTO MECHANIC OF THE RACE AWARD: Jimmy Makar, Interstate Batteries Chevrolet
MAXX RACE CARDS FORMER ROOKIE AWARD: Sterling Marlin, Kodak Film Chevrolet
GOODY'S HEADACHE AWARD: Ken Schrader, Budweiser Chevrolet
CAUTION FLAGS: 7 for 33 laps (74-77, 80-83, 109-113, 153-156, 233-237, 266-270)
LAP LEADERS: Jeff Gordon-pole, Bobby Labonte 1-7, Gordon 8-44, Ken Schrader 45-59, Todd Bodine 60-62, Schrader 63-69,
T. Bodine 70-72, Rusty Wallace 73-84, Rusty Wallace 85-86, B. Labonte 87-114, R. Wallace 115-117, B. Labonte 118-121, R. Wallace
122, Schrader 123-124, R. Wallace 125-128, Dale Earnhardt 129-136, Michael Waltrip 137-145, Sterling Marlin 146-153, Mark
Martin 154-157, Morgan Shepherd 158-164, Earnhardt 165-192, Schrader 193-216, B. Labonte 217-218, Ricky Rudd 219-221,
Schrader 222-266, Marlin 267-289, Schrader 290-291, Earnhardt 292-293, B. Labonte 294, Schrader 295-333, Terry Labonte
334, Schrader 335-357, B. Labonte 358-400.   32 lead changes among 12 drivers.

**TOP 10 NASCAR WINSTON CUP POINTS**

| | | (Wins) |
|---|---|---|
| 1 | -Dale Earnhardt | 1649 (2) |
| | -Mark Martin | 1569 (1) |
| | -Sterling Marlin | 1563 (2) |
| | -Jeff Gordon | 1548 (3) |
| 5 | -Ted Musgrave | 1456 (0) |
| 6 | -Terry Labonte | 1379 (1) |
| 7 | -Bobby Hamilton | 1360 (0) |
| 8 | -Rusty Wallace | 1357 (1) |
| 9 | -Bobby Labonte | 1356 (1) |
| 10 | -Michael Waltrip | 1313 (0) |

**BUSCH POLE AWARD STANDINGS**

| | |
|---|---|
| Jeff Gordon | 5 |
| Dale Earnhardt | 1 |
| Dale Jarrett | 1 |
| Bobby Labonte | 1 |
| Terry Labonte | 1 |
| Mark Martin | 1 |
| cky Rudd | 1 |

**RCA PIT STRATEGY AWARD**

| | Car # | Pts. |
|---|---|---|
| Andy Petree | (# 3) | 3 |
| Ray Evernham | (#24) | 1 |
| Steve Hmiel | (# 6) | 1 |

**UNOCAL 76**
**POINT FUND STANDINGS**

| | |
|---|---|
| Dale Earnhardt | 1649 |
| Sterling Marlin | 1563 |
| Bobby Hamilton | 1360 |

**MAXX RACE CARDS ROOKIE OF THE YEAR**

| | |
|---|---|
| Ricky Craven | 118 |
| Robert Pressley | 115 |
| Randy LaJoie | 107 |
| Davy Jones | 68 |

**SEARS DIEHARD RACER AWARD**

| | (Miles Completed) |
|---|---|
| Bobby Hamilton | 3,942.085 |
| Michael Waltrip | 3,894.269 |
| Brett Bodine | 3,886.938 |

**GATORADE FRONT RUNNER AWARD**

| | |
|---|---|
| Dale Earnhardt | 1649 |
| Mark Martin | 1569 |
| Sterling Marlin | 1563 |

**AP PARTS MEET THE CHALLENGE**

| | Car # | Pts. |
|---|---|---|
| Steve Grissom | (#29) | 77 |
| Geoff Bodine | (# 7) | 34 |
| Ward Burton | (#31) | 32 |

**AE CLEVITE ENGINE BUILDERS OF YEAR**

| | Car # | Pts. |
|---|---|---|
| Charlie Siegars | (#24) | 75 |
| Spenny Clendenen | (# 3) | 69 |
| Randy Hewitt | (# 6) | 66 |

**TRUE VALUE HARD CHARGER**

| | |
|---|---|
| Jeff Gordon | 11,765 |
| Dale Earnhardt | 9,545 |
| Mark Martin | 5,794 |

**MANUFACTURERS' CHAMPIONSHIP**

| | Points | Wins |
|---|---|---|
| Chevrolet | 93 | 9 |
| Ford | 69 | 2 |
| Pontiac | 46 | 0 |

**PLASTI-KOTE QUALITY FINISH AWARD**

| | Car # | Avg Fin |
|---|---|---|
| Andy Petree | (# 3) | 8.72 |
| Tony Glover | (# 4) | 9.54 |
| Steve Hmiel | (# 6) | 10.09 |

**WESTERN AUTO MECHANIC OF YEAR**

| | Car # | Pts. |
|---|---|---|
| Ray Evernham | (#24) | 730 |
| Steve Hmiel | (# 6) | 682 |
| Tony Glover | (# 4) | 651 |

NEXT EVENT: June 4, 1995 - MILLER GENUINE DRAFT 500 - Dover, DE - (500 M) (500 L) $1,254,250

NOTE: The above figures are based on team winnings and include racing purse and cash contingency awards by participating
manufacturers. (1/4/96/tee)

---

Busch Series—the Labonte brothers serve as a bridge between NASCAR eras, their career beginnings separated by eight years.

Quarter-midgets were a family thing, and a lasting thing. Bobby grew up watching the pint-sized, lightning-fast machines and idolizing his older brother, who was already at the wheel. Bobby never forgot. In Salisbury, North Carolina, the North Carolina Quarter Midget Association Speedway thrives thanks to Bobby, who helped finance the project.

Fans will never forget either. They will never forget the dignity and demeanor exuded by Terry off-track, and the calculated smoothness on-track, qualities that led one rather routine nickname—Texas Terry—to be replaced by another—Ice Man. Neither will they forget Bobby's boyish enthusiasm during his championship season. The record books will always be at the ready, to pique those memories.

**LEFT:** Bobby wins! (Terry comes in second.) NASCAR Race Report, May 28, 1995.

Terry (left) and Bob Labonte Sr. in 1993.

OPPOSITE: Kenny Wallace (left) congratulates Bobby on his 1991 NASCAR Series Busch championship.
LEFT: Terry (left) and Bobby become the first NASCAR-champion brothers in 2000.

*The* FAMILY RECORDS

### Terry Labonte
#### (BORN NOVEMBER 16, 1956)

Terry, the eldest Labonte brother, won his first NASCAR NEXTEL Cup championship in 1984. Twelve years later he won the championship again—the longest gap between titles for multiple titlists.

Going into the 2006 season, the "semiretired" driver had twenty-two career victories and twenty-seven poles in 831 starts. Included in that total were the 655 consecutive starts that earned him NASCAR's unofficial "Iron Man" title until the summer of 2000, when injuries ended his streak.

Terry had 181 top-five finishes entering the 2006 season, and 360 top tens—plus career winnings of $39,012,319, the tenth-best prize-money total all-time.

### Bobby Labonte
#### (BORN MAY 8, 1964)

Bobby completed the unique brother quiniela with his championship season in 2000, which followed his second-place finish in 1999. He won four races during 2000.

Bobby started 2006 with twenty-one victories, 110 top fives, 184 top tens, and twenty-six poles. And his career winnings total of $45,690,661 was good for sixth on the all-time list.

He also remains the only driver to win both the NASCAR NEXTEL Cup championship and the NASCAR Busch Series championship, having won the latter in 1991.

### Justin Labonte
#### (BORN FEBRUARY 25, 1981)

Justin, Terry's son, ended the 2005 season with seventy-five starts in the NASCAR Busch Series, and $1,650,900 in winnings. He has one career win, which came on July 10, 2004, at Chicagoland Speedway.

## The FAMILY STORIES

COMING INTO THE 2006 SEASON, IT WAS BY NO MEANS demeaning to Terry Labonte to predict he would never win another NASCAR NEXTEL Cup race. The cadence had changed, and Terry, set to turn fifty in November, was perhaps a bit out of step as a part-time driver slated to split time between two teams, Hendrick Motorsports and the first-year Hall of Fame Racing operation. For many fans of the two-time champion, that was just fine, as their pro-Terry sensibilities were satisfied, knowing that his career was book-ended by victories in one of NASCAR's most hallowed events.

Terry Labonte's first NASCAR NEXTEL Cup victory came at Darlington (South Carolina) Raceway in the Southern 500, on September 1, 1980. What will likely be his last NASCAR NEXTEL Cup victory also came in the Southern 500, on August 31, 2003.

The Southern 500 has since been taken off the schedule, because Darlington is now limited to one race per season, per its sponsorship. But while the Southern 500 existed, it was always one of NASCAR's accepted "majors" because of its status as the schedule's "elder." The Southern 500 was first held in 1950, won by Johnny Mantz in a Plymouth co-owned by NASCAR founder Bill France Sr.

The 1980 season was Terry's third in NASCAR NEXTEL Cup, but only his second full-time campaign. Already, though, his partnership with car owner Billy Hagan was showing promise. A five-race debut in 1978 produced top-ten runs in his first three outings. The very first was—of course—the Southern 500, where he finished fourth.

OPPOSITE: Terry's first cup start in 1978. ABOVE: Terry Labonte and Billy Hagan at the 1984 championship banquet.

In '79, Terry's first full-time effort was a great success. He finished tenth in the final standings, and second in the Rookie of the Year competition to Dale Earnhardt.

The 1980 Southern 500 was used as a backdrop for politicos. Vice-presidential nominee George Bush attended, as did Chip Carter, son of then-president Jimmy Carter. Seven-time series champion Richard Petty, a noted Republican, hobnobbed with Bush, with Bush's people saying Petty had "endorsed" the Ronald Reagan–Bush ticket.

Bush left early for another function. Too bad, because he missed a classic finish. Terry passed three-time series champion David Pearson—Darlington's winningest driver—on the next-to-last lap and went on to win in the No. 44 Apache Classic Stove Chevrolet. Prior to that pass, Terry hadn't led a lap.

Fast forward to a muggy late-summer afternoon in 2003, the last such setting for the Southern 500—it was moved to November in 2004 before leaving the schedule. Those who remembered the 1980 race had to be jolted by its striking similarity to this victory by Terry. Despite running near the front most of the day, he didn't take the lead until Lap 335 of the 367-lap event, after a first-rate pit stop enabled him to move from third to first place.

A great restart got him farther in front of the field, and he ended up winning by fifteen car lengths, snapping a 156-race winless streak dating to the spring of 1999.

Labonte, ever old-school, celebrated like they used to. No donuts, no burnouts. Instead, he had the checkered flag tossed down to him, whereupon he took a single, measured victory lap around NASCAR's oldest oval.

SO, JUST HOW *DO* YOU WIN CHAMPIONSHIPS TWELVE YEARS APART? TIME does not stand still in stock-car racing, that's for sure. Terry Labonte, though, has a style fit for any era, having honed consistency into an accelerated art form. He came into NASCAR racing that way, and will leave NASCAR racing that way.

Exhibit A: His 1984 championship season. Granted, he had only two wins, but twenty-four top tens in thirty starts made up for that over the balance of the season.

**OPPOSITE**: Terry's first and last victories, reflected in his first NASCAR race reports, September 1, 1980, and his last, August 31, 2003. Both wins came at Darlington. **ABOVE**: Bobby Labonte wins at Darlington in 2000. Jimmy Makar, his crew chief, is pictured far left.

Exhibit B: His 1996 championship season. Once again, only two victories. Once again, an inordinate number of laps spent running near the front, yielding another twenty-four top tens in thirty-one starts.

Two sets of statistics, so similar—*that's* how you win championships twelve years apart.

BOBBY LABONTE WAS BOTH CONSISTENT *AND* DOMINANT DURING his NASCAR NEXTEL Cup championship season in 2000. He had four victories during the year, the first coming at the second race on the schedule, in Rockingham, North Carolina. Bobby took the points lead the next week in Las Vegas, and stayed atop the standings the rest of the way with the exception of one week, winning two of the sport's major races—the Brickyard 400 at Indianapolis Motor Speedway and the Southern 500 at Darlington Raceway. His last win of the season came in October, at Lowe's Motor Speedway in Concord, North Carolina.

There had to be some special satisfaction, aside from the title at season's end, when the final standings showed: He had held off the legendary Dale Earnhardt, who finished as series' runner-up, 265 points behind.

Dominance aside, there was a bit of his brother's style in Bobby's championship charge. He had twenty-four top-ten finishes—the same total as Terry had in two championship years. How many times did he fail to finish? Not once.

WELL, WHADDYA KNOW, FOR ONCE TERRY LABONTE FAILED US. HE FAILED to live up to his nickname, "Ice Man."

On a bright summer day at a racetrack that personifies NASCAR's changing landscape, Terry Labonte was emotional, downright choked up.

He had a good reason. He had watched his son, Justin, get his first NASCAR victory, in the Tropicana Twister 300, a NASCAR Busch Series race at Chicagoland Speedway.

"This is bigger than any win I've ever had, to me personally," Terry told reporters afterward.

Justin looked just like the old man, running solidly, steadily, waiting for someone to falter. When leader Mike Wallace, apparently heading for the win, ran out of gas on the last lap, Justin was in the right place, and took advantage.

Forget that this was not NASCAR NEXTEL Cup. Forget that Justin Labonte was no threat in the series championship battle. And forget that his father has two NASCAR NEXTEL Cup titles to his credit.

Forget all that. Terry Labonte did. His son had won his first NASCAR race, and that was all that mattered.

Terry and his son, Justin Labonte.

# The WALTRIPS

OPPOSITE: Darrell poses with his Ford in 1966. ABOVE: Darrell Waltrip runs third in his first race at Daytona in 1966.

"BOOGITY-BOOGITY-BOOGITY" IS A fun phrase, but hopefully Darrell Waltrip's signature expression hasn't overshadowed his real NASCAR notoriety.

He won three NASCAR NEXTEL Cup championships in the 1980s, replacing Richard Petty and Cale Yarborough at the sport's pinnacle. In the process, he became NASCAR's version of Muhammad Ali—without the politics.

Darrell Waltrip was bold and boastful, loud and louder. He was the pioneer of attitude in NASCAR, sending the living legends packing while building his own legend, one victory, one barb, at a time.

Darrell is the leader of what has come to be called the "Owensboro Posse"— derived from his hometown of Owensboro, Kentucky, the humble place where Darrell would watch the weekend short-track races with his grandparents. Those nights inspired bicycle races, then go-karts, then laps around various short tracks in Kentucky and Tennessee.

As he got older and his talent progressed, so did his style; early on, Waltrip sought to entertain by talking in addition to driving. At Waltrip's first race at Nashville Fairgrounds Speedway in the late 1960s, he introduced himself to the track's promoter, Bill Donoho, as "Darrell Waltrip, your next superstar."

Supported by his wife Stevie, who worked in the pits and was one of the first women to be actively involved day-to-day in the NASCAR garage, Waltrip continued to advance his career and reached the NASCAR NEXTEL Cup Series in 1972.

Petty, Yarborough, David Pearson, and Bobby Allison were the "Big Four" back then. The way Waltrip saw it, they had no inclination to make it a Big Five,

BELOW: Stevie Waltrip keeps lap times for Darrell in 1980. RIGHT: Darrell and Stevie in the mid-1970s. OPPOSITE: Darrell and Stevie pose with the 1989 Busch 500 trophy at Bristol.

so he decided to blaze a separate trail, racing fast and talking faster. That combination led to his first nickname, "Jaws," via Yarborough.

"Those guys had a fraternity," Waltrip recalls. "I felt like I was always the odd man out. That motivated me to do better. I had to be outspoken and I had to do things that were not always popular. I was aggressive on the racetrack. All of a sudden I was competing against those guys and they didn't know anything about me; they didn't know if they could trust me.

"I had to earn their respect, but looking back, I didn't give them any, so I probably didn't deserve any. It took a while for that to change but it did."

These days, there is a new nickname, the much friendlier and trendier "DW." But in reality, "Jaws" lives still, reincarnated as a fast-talking FOX network announcer and television commercial costar with younger brother and current driver Michael Waltrip.

DW's trademark "triple-boogity" call at the start of each race broadcast has become as recognizable as "Gentlemen, start your engines."

But years from now, he hopefully will be remembered for what he was—one of NASCAR's greatest champions.

ABOVE: Michael Waltrip in 1965.
OPPOSITE ABOVE: Darrell Waltrip after winning his first championship, in 1981.
OPPOSITE BELOW: Darrell and Stevie.

### Darrell Waltrip
**(BORN FEBRUARY 5, 1947)**

Darrell has eighty-four career victories in NASCAR NEXTEL Cup, tied with Bobby Allison for third-best total all-time. Darrell won three NASCAR NEXTEL Cup championships—1981, '82, and '85, all driving for legendary driver/owner Junior Johnson. Darrell won the Daytona 500 in 1989, in his seventeenth try. Darrell was incredibly dominant during 1981 and '82 championship runs, with a total of twenty-four victories, thirty-eight top-five finishes, forty-five top tens, and eighteen poles. Darrell was also named one of NASCAR's 50 Greatest Drivers.

### Stevie Waltrip
**(BORN JULY 7, 1950)**

Stevie was one of the first women to work in the pits during NASCAR races, and as a result she is viewed as a trailblazer in terms of women in NASCAR who weren't drivers. Her important task for a number of years was to carefully track the laps her husband Darrell was turning during races. She became a role model, and in the mid-1980s women increasingly started becoming involved both along pit road and in the garage area.

### Michael Waltrip
**(BORN APRIL 30, 1963)**

Michael, Darrell's younger brother, is a two-time Daytona 500 champion (2001 and '03). His first 500 victory ended a 462-race winless streak in NASCAR NEXTEL Cup. In 1996, Michael had his first big breakthrough in the NASCAR NEXTEL All-Star Challenge, a non-points race. He started the 2006 season with four victories in NASCAR NEXTEL Cup, and eleven in the NASCAR Busch Series.

**LEFT:** Darrell Waltrip (in No. 95) in his first NASCAR NEXTEL Cup start, the 1972 Winston 500. **OPPOSITE:** Darrell doing the "Icky Shuffle" after his victory at the 1989 Daytona 500.

DARRELL WALTRIP STARTED OFF HIS NASCAR NEXTEL CUP CAREER riding in style on May 9, 1972, at Talladega Superspeedway. Forget the fact that he started in the middle of the pack at number twenty-five, and finished back in the pack, in thirty-eighth. Just recall that he was in one of the coolest cars in NASCAR history—the one driven by none other than Mario Andretti when he won the 1967 Daytona 500.

The car was a Holman-Moody "house car," a machine shared by a variety of drivers. Most notably, Bobby Allison drove it to his first superspeedway win, at North Carolina Speedway in 1967. It originally was a Ford Fairlane, but by the time Waltrip drove it, it had evolved into a 1971 Mercury.

DARRELL WAS DANCING IN VICTORY LANE ON THE AFTERNOON of February 19, 1989, when the thirty-first annual Daytona 500 had been completed. He was doing an impromptu mimicking of the "Icky Shuffle," the celebratory touchdown dance made popular by Cincinnati Bengals running back Icky Woods.

Were the stars aligned for this DW breakthrough? Hard to say, but most certainly the numbers were aligned.

Darrell's car number was seventeen; so was his pit-stall number; and of course, 1989 marked his seventeenth attempt at winning the Daytona 500.

It was an opportunistic win. Ken Schrader led 114 of the race's 200 laps, with Waltrip hanging around back in the pack. With ten laps remaining, Schrader and Dale Earnhardt, running first and second, pitted for gas; Darrell, driving the Tide-sponsored Chevrolet owned by Rick Hendrick—the original "Tide Machine"—decided to stay out, and gambled.

Running second behind Alan Kulwicki, Waltrip took over the lead on Lap 196 when Kulwicki's car slowed. The gamble paid off, but it could have easily backfired.

"Those last four laps, I think I had four heart attacks," Waltrip said.

OPPOSITE: Michael Waltrip is congratulated after winning the 1983 Goody's Dash race at Darlington. ABOVE: Michael Waltrip in Victory Lane after winning the 1996 all-star race.

MICHAEL WALTRIP IS KNOWN TO BE A BIT ZANY, WHICH HAS SERVED him well in his budding second career as a NASCAR television personality, again following his brother's lead. For example, after winning a NASCAR Busch Series race at Bristol Motor Speedway in Tennessee, in April 1993, he produced an engagement ring and wedding proposal for future wife, Buffy, in Victory Lane. Moments before he had done a celebration "Polish Victory Lap"—going the wrong way around the half-mile oval—to honor his good friend Alan Kulwicki, who had died earlier that week in a plane crash en route to Bristol.

Michael said later that none of those post-race activities had been planned ahead of time.

Said Michael: "It was emotional, you know?"

MICHAEL WALTRIP'S NASCAR NEXTEL CUP WINLESS STREAK STOOD at 309 races coming into the annual all-star weekend in May 1996. When Waltrip arrived at Lowe's Motor Speedway on the afternoon of May 18, he wasn't even in the all-star race—then called the Winston Select—field. Being a nonwinner, he was relegated to the preliminary, called the Winston Select Open, which awarded the top five finishers berths in the big race.

Michael finished fifth, barely making it—and then barely had time to celebrate, as he had to hustle to prepare for the all-star battle.

Entering the last of the race's three segments, Waltrip found himself in good position. And when he slid by the cars of Dale Earnhardt and Terry Labonte, who had collided slightly while battling for the lead, he found himself in great position. Michael said afterward that he was expecting such an incident to take place, given the competitive nature of the two former series champions.

Older brother Darrell admitted he never thought about Michael winning the event. But he also admitted something else, after being told over the radio what had transpired.

Said Darrell: "I couldn't wait to get out there to Victory Lane and congratulate him."

TALK ABOUT CRUEL IRONY. MICHAEL FINALLY HAD HIS BREAKTHROUGH NASCAR NEXTEL Cup win on February 18, 2001, winning the Daytona 500. After taking the checkered flag, he learned that he had crossed the finish line only moments after his car's owner, seven-time series champion Dale Earnhardt, had crashed and died in Turn 4.

Up in the broadcast booth, Darrell was working the race for FOX, the first race of the new landmark television rights deal between the network and NASCAR. Viewers heard the joy in Darrell's voice, because his brother had won. They also heard the concern as he looked out toward the crash site, and wondered aloud about the fate of his old friend and rival.

Two years later, Michael won the 500 again, only this time there was another sidebar issue. The race was halted prematurely, after 109 laps, because of rain.

While one celebration had been ruined by tragedy, this one had been tainted by a statistical asterisk. Waltrip handled both situations professionally, and, in the case of the '03 victory, he was able to fend off inquiring media with humor.

During the post-race press conference in the Daytona International Speedway press box, high above a soaked tri-oval, Waltrip was asked a couple of questions about whether the rainout would ruin the victory. Suddenly he said, "Wait. You know what I just heard? They're still going to pay me the full amount for winning.

"Crazy, isn't it?"

ABOVE: Michael Waltrip wins the 2001 Daytona 500. BELOW: Darrell (left) and Michael Waltrip (1991). OPPOSITE: Michael and Buffy Waltrip with the 2003 Daytona 500 trophy.

# *The* EARNHARDTS

OPPOSITE: Ralph in the mid-1950s behind the wheel of No. 8. ABOVE: Ralph Earnhardt (left) wins the NASCAR Sportsman Division title in 1956.

SEVEN-TIME NASCAR NEXTEL CUP Series champions Dale Earnhardt and Richard Petty have something other than that all-time record in common. They also both had fathers who had their own fabulous racing careers, but who were overshadowed by their sons.

That's especially true with Kannapolis, North Carolina's, Ralph Lee Earnhardt. To this day, some will swear that he is the greatest dirt-track stock-car driver in history, regardless of the sanctioning body's acronym.

Ralph won NASCAR's Sportsman Division title in 1956, and between 1956 and '64, he ran a smattering of NASCAR NEXTEL Cup (then called Grand National) races, fifty-one to be exact, posting sixteen top-ten finishes.

Driving self-prepared cars adorned with the No. 8, which his grandson Dale Earnhardt Jr. has made a national phenomenon, Ralph preferred to run the short tracks out of the limelight, racing to win and put food in the fridge.

In 1956, in addition to the NASCAR Sportsman title, he also claimed six different track Sportsman championships; finished second in points at two other tracks; and finished as runner-up in the North Carolina State Sportsman point standings, only six behind Ned Jarrett, whom he'd edged to win the NASCAR Sportsman crown. And finally, he also won the South Carolina State Sportsman championship.

**ABOVE:** A restored car of Ralph's. **RIGHT:** Dale Earnhardt, circa 1972.
**OPPOSITE:** Ralph Earnhardt after a win at Hickory in the 1950s.

Hickory Motor Speedway in Hickory, North Carolina, was his home track, as it was for many of yesteryear's stars, including two-time NASCAR NEXTEL Cup champion Jarrett. Ralph raced to five Hickory track championships (in 1953, '54, '56, '57, and '59). He had a streak of seventeen feature victories there.

Those seventeen were only part of several hundred victories by Ralph overall on short tracks, victories that formed a legacy and a lineage. He died in 1973, at the age of forty-five. Had he lived, there doubtless would've been more victories.

But he was destined to be an afterthought for NASCAR's future generation of fans. That's what happens when you're followed on the family tree by someone larger than life.

And if anyone had ever doubted that Dale Earnhardt—whose given full name was Ralph Dale Earnhardt—was indeed larger than life, they probably changed their mind in the days immediately following his death on February 18, 2001, after an accident on the last lap of the Daytona 500.

The outpouring of national sympathy was overwhelming, and immediately transformed his son, Dale Earnhardt Jr., into perhaps the most popular driver in the history of NASCAR, with the possible exception of Richard Petty.

The FAMILY RECORDS

OPPOSITE: Ralph, in 1961. LEFT: Dale Sr. wins the first NASCAR Busch Series race, the Goody's 300, in 1982.

### Ralph Earnhardt

**(FEBRUARY 23, 1928–SEPTEMBER 26, 1973)**

Ralph was the NASCAR Sportsman Division champion in 1956, and raced fifty-one times in NASCAR NEXTEL Cup (at the time, the Grand National Cup), with six top-five finishes and sixteen top tens. One highlight took place during his first try at the big time, on November 11, 1956, at Hickory Motor Speedway, in the Buddy Shuman 250. Driving for Pete DePaolo-owned Ford, he finished second behind Speedy Thompson. His busiest premier-series season was 1962, racing in seventeen of the series' fifty-three races. His best finish that season was a third place at Concord (North Carolina) Speedway. Ralph was named one of NASCAR's 50 Greatest Drivers in 1998.

### Dale Earnhardt

**(APRIL 29, 1951–FEBRUARY 18, 2001)**

Dale won seven NASCAR NEXTEL Cup titles (1980, '86, '87, '90, '91, '93, '94), tying the record previously established by Richard Petty. He won seventy-six NASCAR NEXTEL Cup races between 1975 and 2000, the sixth-best total all-time. Dale is the all-time leader in Daytona International Speedway victories, with thirty-four; that total includes one Daytona 500 win, in 1998. He was the three-time runner-up in the final series championship standings; won twenty-one NASCAR Busch Series races, including the series' inaugural race, in February 1982, at Daytona; and won the International Race of Champions Series four times (1990, '95, '99, 2000). Dale was also named one of NASCAR's 50 Greatest Drivers.

### Kerry Earnhardt
#### (BORN DECEMBER 8, 1969)

Kerry, Dale Jr.'s older half-brother, made sixty-eight NASCAR Busch Series starts between 1998 and 2005, running a full schedule of thirty-four races in 2002, and finishing twenty-second in the point standings. He has three top-five finishes and six top tens in the series. He also made seven NASCAR NEXTEL Cup starts between 2000 and 2005, and started 2006 driving full-time in the NASCAR Craftsman Truck Series.

### Kelley Earnhardt
#### (BORN AUGUST 28, 1972)

Kelley, Dale Jr.'s older sister, raced Late Model stock cars while attending college at the University of North Carolina–Charlotte. Today she is the president of JR Motorsports in Mooresville, North Carolina.

### Dale Earnhardt Jr.
#### (BORN OCTOBER 10, 1974)

Dale Jr. came into the 2006 season with sixteen NASCAR NEXTEL Cup Series victories. He joined the series full-time in 2002, after a five-race debut in 1999. Dale Jr. finished third in NASCAR NEXTEL Cup final point standings in 2003 and fifth in 2004, the year he started off by winning the Daytona 500. He won the NASCAR Busch Series championship in 1998 and '99.

Dale Earnhardt Sr. and Jr. at Talladega, 2000.

**RIGHT:** Dale Jr. poses with (left to right) Dale Sr., stepmother Teresa, and sister Kelley at the 1998 NASCAR Busch Series championship team trophy ceremony. **BELOW:** Dale Jr.'s 1998 NASCAR Busch Series championship team, with Dale Sr., Teresa, and crew.

OPPOSITE: Dale Sr.'s first Cup start, May 1975. ABOVE: Dale Jr. driving on the outside in one of his first races.

YEARS AGO, WHEN ASSESSING THE STOCK CAR RACING POTENTIAL OF his sons, Dale Earnhardt used to surprise people by saying his daughter Kelley, who was running in Late Model stock cars at the time, was a better racer than either of his sons. Funny how things work out. There was a time when Dale Jr. built Late Models for his sister. Now she manages his busy appearance schedule.

RALPH'S CARS ALWAYS WORE THE NO. 8, AS DALE JR.'S DO NOW. WHEN Dale Sr. made his NASCAR NEXTEL Cup debut in the 1975 World 600, the Ed Negre-owned Dodge he drove also was the No. 8. Dale finished a very respectable twenty-second. But Dale Sr. could probably race well in just about anything. Says Dale Jr., "My father would take something that other guys would probably throw away, fix it and make it run, and outrun the other guys with it. Dad always taught us to do the best with what we had, and that's what I've always done."

AN EPIC DAY FOR THE EARNHARDT FAMILY OCCURRED AUGUST 20, 2000, at the Pepsi 400 at Michigan International Speedway. Dale Sr., Dale Jr., and Kerry all were in a NASCAR field for the first time. On being on the track with his father, Dale Jr. says, "To see him next to you and being in competition for position was a lot of fun. It's something that you don't know exactly how it's gonna make you feel until you get out there, and then you're overcome with some sense of acceptance and accomplishment because he's the ultimate. It's something you get right away as a kid, to do what he's doing and be like him."

Unfortunately, that August race turned out to be the only time the three Earnhardt men raced together. Dale Sr. finished sixth, Dale Jr. thirty-first, and Kerry forty-third.

ABOVE: Dale Sr. (center) with son Kerry Earnhardt (left) after Kerry's ARCA win at Pocono.
OPPOSITE: On his twentieth attempt, Dale wins the 1998 Daytona 500.

KERRY EARNHARDT WON FOUR ARCA RACES BEFORE GETTING HIS SHOT at the NASCAR big time, and there always has been the belief that if he ever won races his popularity would rival his brother's. After all, the facial resemblance to his father is uncanny. His voice is also very reminiscent—as is his playful demeanor. And, despite his uneven results thus far, he already has been well received by fans throughout the country.

"It's been amazing, all the support they've given me," Kerry says. "They've stayed behind me the whole time I've been racing. It's great to hear the response from the crowd when you walk across the stage for driver introductions, or when you're walking to your car along pit road before qualifying. The fans are always hollering and screaming at me. It's pretty cool, that support.

"I love racing. It's in my blood, I suppose you could say. But at the same time, I've come to learn that life is about a lot more than racing."

FINALLY, IT HAPPENED. ON FEBRUARY 15, 1998, ONE OF THE MOST puzzling runs in the history of racing—in the history of sport, really—ended, as Dale Earnhardt won the Daytona 500 on his twentieth try.

Until then, the driver with the most Daytona International Speedway victories had been continually frustrated. Once, a sure win was negated by a last-lap flat tire. Another time, a seagull, caught in the grille of his Chevy, messed things up late in the race. And another occasion saw NASCAR's best driver run out of gas down the stretch.

Even this victory in 1998 had a touch of the absurd, as it came under a caution period, adding an anticlimactic accent to one of NASCAR's greatest moments. But drama returned immediately after he took the checkered flag, as members of every pit crew rushed out to pit road during his victory lap, ready for a massive reception as he rolled by on his way to Victory Lane.

What a picture: the No. 3 Goodwrench Chevy going down pit road, Earnhardt's left arm out the window, touching and shaking hand after hand. Moments later, in Victory Lane, Earnhardt climbed atop his car for a celebratory pose.

Off the car, arm-in-arm with wife Teresa, he stepped into the hearts of America as he talked to CBS announcer Ken Squier. He thanked a variety of people. And to his late father, his mother Martha, and his children, he offered this:

"I love you all."

This, from the man they called "The Intimidator."

IF EMOTIONS RAN HIGH ON THE DAY DALE SR. WON THE 500, IT WAS nothing compared to the night of July 7, 2001.

Dale Sr. had been dead less than five months, and the NASCAR NEXTEL Cup Series was back at Daytona International Speedway.

Of course, Dale Earnhardt Jr. won. Dry eyes were rare in the crowd of more than 150,000 as the No. 8 Budweiser Chevrolet was parked at the start-finish

line, its driver standing on top, then leaping, mosh pit–like, into the arms of onrushing crew members.

Dale Jr. admitted that he would cry at some point that night, sooner or later. But first, he had to do his dad right.

"I dedicate this win to him," the son said. "There's nobody else."

It was time for another dedication, on February 15, 2004: Dale Jr. won the Daytona 500, and all the emotions of 2001 came rushing back.

It wasn't all bad, though. The passage of time had provided some healing, and the son was able to talk about pride instead of pain. He talked about all the years his father tried to win the 500 without success.

"There were not many things that ate that man's insides out, but losing this race over and over, you could see it on his face," Dale Jr. said. "And inside of me, that started the desire to win this race.

"I'll be honest. This race is more important to me than anything." As if anyone should ever be surprised at that.

And so the Earnhardt legacy indeed lives on. Kerry tried to explain what it means: "Being a member of the Earnhardt family does put pressure on you sometimes, because there always are—and always will be—expectations of you because of the name.

"But many other times, being a member of the Earnhardt family . . . is just kind of cool."

OPPOSITE LEFT: In 1998, Ralph and Dale were both included among NASCAR's 50 greatest drivers. OPPOSITE RIGHT: A ticket to the Dale Earnhardt tribute concert at Daytona, June 28, 2003. ABOVE: Dale Jr. and Sr. in 2000.

DAVID PEAR

# The PEARSONS

OPPOSITE: David with his wife, Helen, and sons Larry (left) and Ricky, celebrate winning the 1961 Firecracker 250. ABOVE: David Pearson's 1968 championship trophy.

GREATEST NASCAR NEXTEL CUP driver ever? As hard as it might be for some fans to accept, not everyone automatically invokes the names Petty or Earnhardt when faced with this question.

There is an undercurrent in NASCAR Nation, a ripple emanating from nostalgic, older fans who prefer to point to another star, the man they called the Silver Fox, who many will tell you is the gold standard when it comes to stock-car driving excellence: David Pearson.

Sure, he won only three championships. But don't forget, he raced only *four* full seasons. He was a capricious competitor, chasing big-time race wins and personal satisfaction more than series championships and mass acclaim.

Much of the time, everyone was chasing David Pearson. Although, looking back, it's important to note that the Spartanburg, South Carolina, native

chose to be a front-runner when it counted—near the end, or at the very end—of a race.

An incredibly popular driver with the fans, David had a style that has been described in general terms as smooth. But if you want to talk specifics, you need to talk about a driver who was smart like, well, a fox. David's formula for success often called for a mixture of back-in-the-pack cruising and late-race charging. He actually was a conservative driver, carefully "saving" his race cars, while others around him either crashed or suffered mechanical problems.

His was a style that clearly worked, to the tune of 105 victories and inclusion on NASCAR's 50 Greatest Drivers list.

Here's another question: Who is the best NASCAR Busch Series driver ever? How about Larry Pearson?

ABOVE: David and Ricky Pearson pose with the 1968 trophy at North Wilkesboro, N.C.; OPPOSITE ABOVE: David gives his son Larry some advice. OPPOSITE BELOW: Ricky (left) and David Pearson, 1987.

That's a credible conclusion. Larry, David's son, was one of the dominant drivers during the series' first decade, the 1980s, winning consecutive titles in 1986 and 1987.

David's other two sons, by the way, are making their own marks in NASCAR. Ricky Pearson started the 2006 season as crew chief for Tim Sauter in the NASCAR Busch Series, with his son, Ricky Jr., serving as a mechanic and tire specialist. Eddie Pearson started 2006 as a mechanic and front-tire changer for Dennis Setzer, one of the top drivers in the NASCAR Craftsman Truck Series.

While the best-ever status of David and Larry Pearson is of course debatable, one thing is certain: They form one of the greatest father-son NASCAR driving duos.

LEFT: (left to right) David, Larry, and Ricky Pearson at Darlington in 1968. BELOW: (left to right) Larry, David, Eddie, and Ricky, in 1982. OPPOSITE: A postcard showing the Dodge Dart David Pearson drove in drag races in 1965, during Chrysler's boycott. Car owner Cotton Owens is on the right.

The COTTON PICKER

Cotton Owens

### David Pearson
#### (BORN DECEMBER 22, 1934)

David had 105 victories in the NASCAR NEXTEL Cup Series, the second-best total of all time, trailing only the two hundred of Richard Petty. The Rookie of the Year in 1960, he gave fans a glimpse of his greatness in '61, when he won several big events, including the World 600 at Charlotte. He raced from 1960 to 1986, making 574 starts, with 301 top-five finishes and 366 top tens. David's prime was from 1964 to 1969, when he won all three of his series titles (1966, '68, and '69). Actually, there were two "primes": between 1972 and 1976 he won thirty-seven races. He drove for some of NASCAR's most legendary owners, such as Cotton Owens, Ray Fox, Holman-Moody, and the Wood Brothers.

### Larry Pearson
#### (BORN NOVEMBER 2, 1953)

Larry, David's son, had his shot in NASCAR NEXTEL Cup, making fifty-seven starts between 1986 and 1991 with three top-ten finishes. His best finish was sixth, and he did that twice—in the autumn of 1987 at Lowe's Motor Speedway, and in the 1989 Richmond spring race. He is clearly one of the very best NASCAR Busch Series drivers of all time, with consecutive championship years of 1986 and 1987, preceded in 1985 and followed in '88 by third-place finishes. During that four-year run, Larry won twelve races and showed championship-caliber consistency, with a total of seventy-nine top-ten finishes. He also had twelve poles during his NASCAR Busch Series career. His two championships were secured in disparate fashion: In 1986, Larry edged Brett Bodine by only twenty points in the final standings; and in 1987, fueled by a series-high six victories after having only one win the year before, Larry outdistanced runner-up Jimmy Hensley by 382 points.

THE *First* ANNUAL

WORLD 600

CHARLOTTE MOTOR SPEEDWAY
HOME OF THE "WORLD 600"

OFFICIAL PROGRAM

PRICE 1.00

DAVID PEARSON'S FIRST NASCAR NEXTEL CUP VICTORY CAME in the 1961 World 600, the race now known as the Coca-Cola 600. What is often forgotten is that David was actually brought in by car owner Ray Fox as a replacement for regular driver Darel Dieringer, who had a contractual conflict because Fox had switched tire companies. David's victory in the Pontiac immediately made *him* Fox's full-time driver.

The victory also led to a classic quote in Victory Lane. The track announcer asked David if he would like to give his pit crew some credit. Pearson declined, but not because he was being selfish about the limelight. "This is my first race with this team," David said, "and I don't know those boys' names."

Looking back years later, David added: "It was May 28, 1961. That's the day I became a full-time race car driver."

WHAT WAS THE GREATEST DAYTONA 500 EVER? IT'S HARD TO ARGUE against 1976, when David and archrival Richard Petty got tangled up coming out of Turn 4 of the last lap, after they had traded slingshot passes, David's coming in Turn 3.

Petty actually never completed his pass. But he thought he did, and started guiding the No. 43, red-and-blue STP Dodge toward the outside of the track—making contact with David's No. 21, red-white-and-gold Purolator Mercury. The impact sent both cars spinning nose-first into the concrete retaining wall, bouncing off, and rolling into the grass bordering the racing surface.

With dirt flying, dust clearing, and 150,000 or so spectators watching, the two machines sat, agonizingly close to the finish line, but going nowhere. There was one significant difference between the two cars, though. Petty's was stalled. David's was running, as he had kept the clutch engaged throughout the spinout.

With Petty frantically trying to refire his car to no avail, David eased the Mercury into first gear and cruised slowly past the finish line. Petty got there eventually, by repeatedly trying to start the car, causing it to lurch slightly forward each time.

Said David: "It must have been some finish to watch, huh?" It was indeed.

THAT WORLD 600 VICTORY IN 1961 WASN'T THE ONLY TIME DAVID became a "super-sub."

At the 1979 Southern 500, Dale Earnhardt was out of action, due to a shoulder injury suffered earlier that season in a Pocono Raceway crash. Pearson took over the Rod Osterlund–owned No. 2 Chevrolet—yes, Earnhardt's number was 2 back then—and won by a daunting two-lap margin at venerable Darlington Raceway.

The next time NASCAR rolled into Darlington—the following spring for the CRC Chemicals 500—it did so without Donnie Allison, who had lost his Hoss Ellington–owned ride. Pearson reported for duty again, and drove the No. 1 Hawaiian Tropic Chevrolet to victory.

**OPPOSITE LEFT:** The program cover from David Pearson's first win, May 28, 1961. **OPPOSITE RIGHT:** David racing toward that first victory, at Charlotte, North Carolina. **LEFT:** David Pearson's accident (left) at the 1976 Daytona 500, which he won.

*Memorabilia*

A color postcard featuring Larry and David Pearson. • A David Pearson Chattanooga Chew Racing Team sticker from the early 1980s.

**ABOVE**: Larry Pearson racing with his father's number and paint job. **RIGHT**: Larry wins at Darlington in 1995. **OPPOSITE**: Larry with his family and crew celebrate his 1987 NASCAR Busch Series championship in Martinsville, Virginia.

FOLLOWING A LEGEND'S FOOTSTEPS IN PROFESSIONAL SPORTS IS A tough task. When that legend is your father, it's even tougher.

Larry Pearson walked that walk, trying to make his own mark in NASCAR. And he walked well, winning those back-to-back NASCAR Busch Series titles. His talent and his name increased credibility for the series in its early years.

Larry also got his shot at the NASCAR NEXTEL Cup. He didn't do so well, driving a family-owned car in 1989, and so he returned to the NASCAR Busch Series.

As his career wound down, the victories were fewer. By 1995, Larry was forty-two years old, and hadn't challenged for the series championship since '88. In that '95 season, though, he rebounded, and was headed toward a top-ten points finish. But first, that spring, he headed toward Darlington Raceway.

His dad's shadow loomed especially large at Darlington. David had won ten races and twelve poles there, records that stand to this day. Nearly seven years

had passed since Larry had won a race anywhere. Also, Larry had never won a race on a superspeedway, and he had never won at Darlington, an issue that Larry said he and his father had, well, "discussed" a number of times.

But finally, in 1995, Larry crossed the finish line about two car lengths ahead of Johnny Benson and got the victory. And later in the season he won again, this time at Myrtle Beach—his last NASCAR Busch Series triumph.

SOME THINGS NEVER CHANGE. DAVID PEARSON IS STILL RACING, driving in a "legends" series on dirt tracks—and winning, competing at times against one of his former car owners, Cotton Owens. Larry, meanwhile, is also still driving, although a lot slower than he used to. He runs the Pearson Driving School in Boiling Springs, South Carolina, teaching safe driving techniques to high school students.

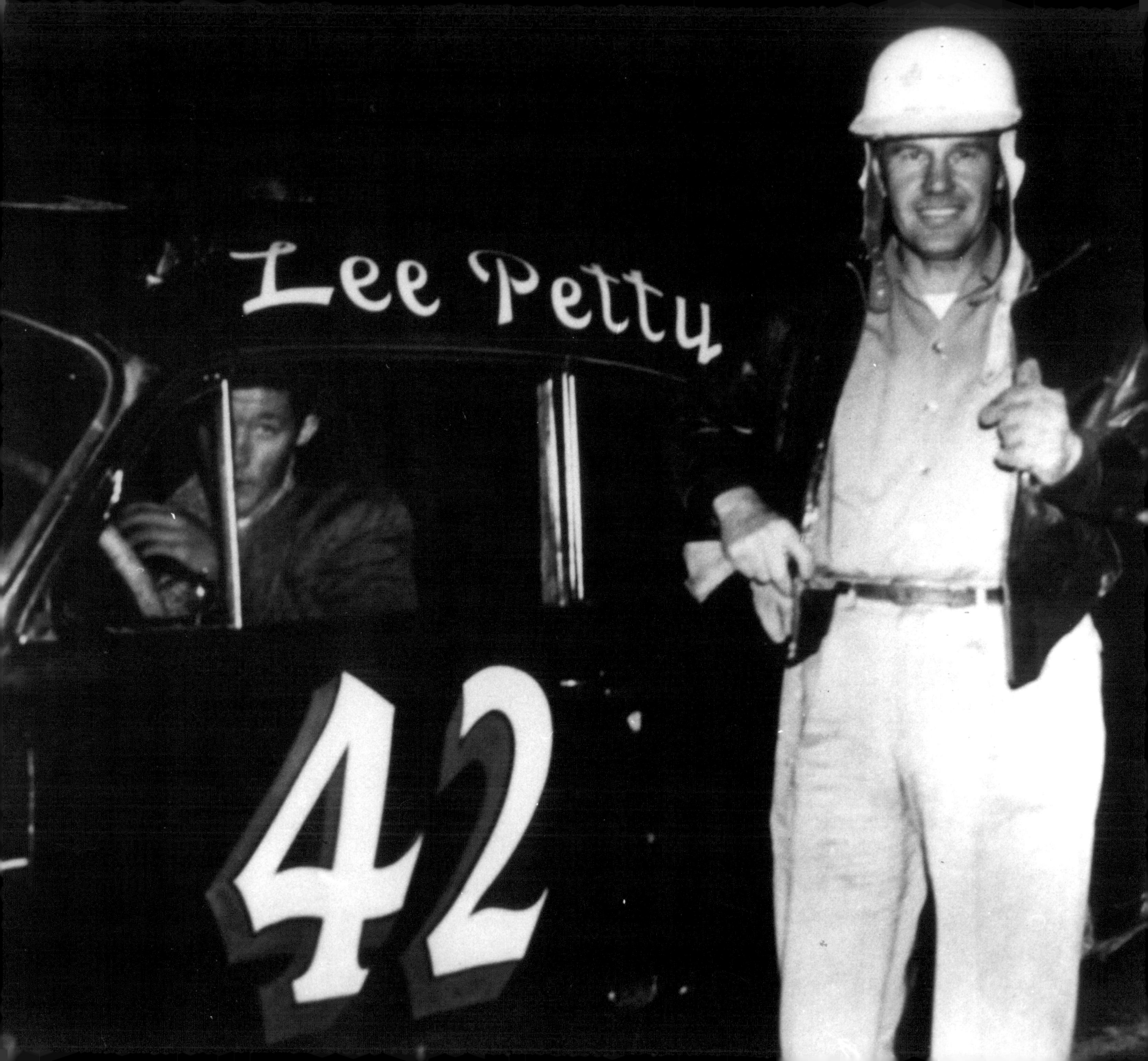
Lee Petty
42

# *The* PETTYS

OPPOSITE: Richard (in car) and Lee Petty, 1953. **ABOVE**: Lee Petty, fourth on the inside, competes in the first Strictly Stock race, 1949.

THOUGH THE KING MAY NO LONGER rule, he does still loom, with his trademark outfit—cowboy hat, sunglasses, jeans, and boots—a welcome throwback to another NASCAR era.

Richard Petty—inactive in terms of driving, but iconic as ever—has been part of the NASCAR scene from the start. As a kid, he watched his father, Lee, set a standard of excellence beginning with the very first season of the NASCAR NEXTEL Cup Series—then called Strictly Stock—in 1949.

Lee Petty: the man who raised a king. He too was NASCAR royalty. Lee won three championships—the first driver to do so—before his boy won even the first of his eventual, all-time record seven. Lee held the record for wins with fifty-four, a mark also broken by Richard en route to another all-time mark: two hundred victories. Richard won the Daytona 500 seven times, also a record, but long before that, Lee won the very first 500, in 1959.

Furthermore, Lee raced in the very first premier series event, at Charlotte Speedway in 1949. He caused the very first caution in series history in that race, rolling a *borrowed* Buick Roadmaster. He had the very first fan club, started by Morris Metcalf, who one day would become NASCAR's chief scorer.

The beginnings were humble. Prize money was minimal. Petty Enterprises was a gleam in Lee's eye—no more than a house and a garage in Randleman, North Carolina. It was a family piled into a car that was driven down the street as well as around the track. Petty Enterprises was a picnic-basket lunch alongside a Southeastern country road.

"We started when I was about eleven years old; we went everywhere," Richard says. "We got to go all over the United States. We'd get hungry and we'd stop, fix some peanut butter sandwiches—we took Mother along to fix supper. Daddy never had a pit crew or any of that kind of stuff. He just went."

Times changed.

"First thing you know, we got a pickup truck, then a trailer, then a truck, and then all kinds of stuff," says Richard. "It just grew." Along with Richard, younger brother Maurice would also find success, making his mark as a crew chief and engine builder, as well as having sixteen top-ten NASCAR NEXTEL Cup finishes between 1960 and '64—in only twenty-six starts.

**OPPOSITE (CLOCKWISE FROM ABOVE LEFT):** Earliest known photo of Lee Petty racing, circa 1948; a young Richard Petty looks on as his father's car is serviced, 1950; Lee drives on (No. 42), 1950. **ABOVE:** Lee with his wife, Elizabeth, at Daytona Beach, 1953. **RIGHT:** 1956 Telefax noting Lee's 25th win.

*Telefax* **WESTERN UNION** *Telefax*
SENDING BLANK

| CALL LETTERS | NA | PD | | CHARGE TO | NASCAR | JULY 2, 1956 | BOOK |

Mervin Hyman, Sports Illustrated, 9 Rockefeller Plaza, NY.NY.
and
Ed Elliott, National Pit Pass, 2808 S. La Cienega, Los Angeles, Calif.
and
Red Phillips, Columbus Star, Columbus, Ohio

Lee Petty won NASCAR Grand National Championship race at Weaverville, N.C. Sunday in Dodge; followed by Jim Paschal, Merc; Joe Eubanks, Ford; Gwyn Staley, Chev; Herb Thomas, ~~Srjorys Sksrgss~~ Chry.300; Fireball Roberts was fastest Qualifier.

Tom Pistone won NASCAR Convertible Championship race at Chicago, Ill. Saturday in Chev; followed by Curtis Turner, Ford; Bill Lutz, Ford; Larry Odo, Chev; Jim Massey, Chev; Curtis Turner was fastest Qualifier.

*Send the above message, subject to the terms on back hereof, which are hereby agreed to*

**PLEASE TYPE OR WRITE PLAINLY WITHIN BORDER—DO NOT FOLD**

Along the way, in addition to setting standards, Lee Petty set examples, mainly about how to get along with people. He enjoyed enormous popularity among both his racing peers and racing fans. Is there any wonder that Richard became one of the most prolific autograph signers in the history of professional sports?

What Lee passed on, so did Richard—to son Kyle, a successful driver in his own right. Dad's the King, but the kid's a prince, one of the garage's most articulate spokesmen, and one of the most approachable. Kyle has become nearly as beloved to fans as Richard, because of the dignified diligence he has shown in honoring the memory of his son, Adam, heir apparent to the family racing legacy, who died in a 2000 accident at New Hampshire International Speedway.

Kyle and his wife, Pattie, have memorialized Adam in the best way possible: by establishing the Victory Junction Gang Camp in Randleman, North Carolina. The camp is geared toward children with life-threatening illnesses; the original idea was Adam's.

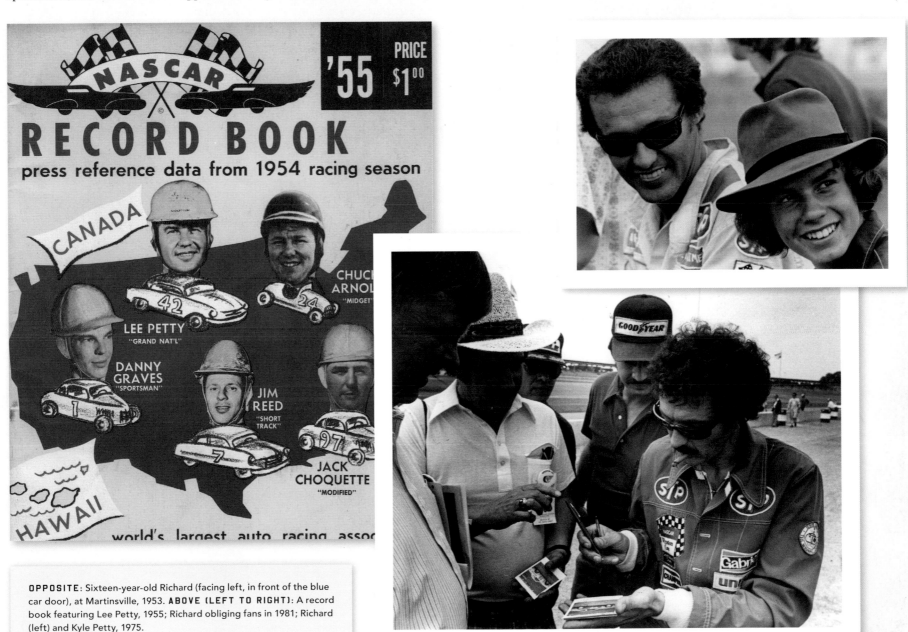

OPPOSITE: Sixteen-year-old Richard (facing left, in front of the blue car door), at Martinsville, 1953. ABOVE (LEFT TO RIGHT): A record book featuring Lee Petty, 1955; Richard obliging fans in 1981; Richard (left) and Kyle Petty, 1975.

OPPOSITE: Richard (left) and Lee, 1960. ABOVE: Richard Petty, reading to his children, circa 1970. RIGHT: Richard (left) and Maurice Petty in Martinsville, Virginia, 1966.

### Lee Petty

#### (MARCH 14, 1914–APRIL 5, 2000)

Lee was the first three-time champion of NASCAR's top series, winning titles in 1954, '58, and '59. He also finished as series runner-up twice: in 1949 and '53. Lee won the first Daytona 500 in 1959, and went on to win fifty-four NASCAR NEXTEL Cup races, the ninth-best all-time total. He had 332 top-ten finishes in 427 starts, and competed full-time for twelve seasons, never finishing a season out of the point standings' top ten. In 1998, Lee was named one of NASCAR's 50 Greatest Drivers. Lee Petty didn't start racing until the age of thirty-five, during a time when mid-thirties was considered retirement territory. He started racing after earning a living as a farmer, and as operator of a trucking company.

### Julian "Julie" Petty

#### (BORN APRIL 1, 1916)

Julian, Lee's brother, made only three NASCAR national series starts himself—one in 1952, two in '55. But as a car owner, he had a laundry list of legendary drivers: Jim Paschal, Bob Welborn, Tiny Lund, Junior Johnson, Marvin Panch, David Pearson, Rex White, and Joe Weatherly. His cars were in 178 NASCAR NEXTEL Cup races, with 13 victories, 14 poles, 68 top fives, and 113 top tens. Welborn also drove a Julie-owned Chevrolet to the 1958 NASCAR Convertible Division championship.

### Richard Petty

#### (BORN JULY 2, 1937)

Richard, Lee's son and NASCAR's ultimate record holder, heads the all-time NASCAR NEXTEL Cup list in victories (200), championships (7, a record shared with Dale Earnhardt), poles (126), starts (1,185),

**ABOVE:** Kyle Petty's parents and grandparents surround him after his 1979 ARCA win at Daytona. **RIGHT:** Julian Petty. **OPPOSITE LEFT:** Ritchie Petty. **OPPOSITE RIGHT:** Kyle Petty leads a Victory Junction Gang fundraiser at Lowe's Motor Speedway.

season victory total (27 in 1967), and consecutive wins (10 in 1967), plus most Daytona 500 victories (7). He was, obviously, named one of NASCAR's 50 Greatest Drivers.

## Maurice Petty
### (BORN MARCH 27, 1939)

Maurice, Lee's youngest son, made twenty-six starts in NASCAR NEXTEL Cup between 1960 and '64, with seven top fives and sixteen top tens. His most active season was 1961, when he raced nine of fifty-two races, with four top tens. His best result was also in 1961, a third-place finish in Spartanburg, South Carolina. For years, Maurice was a crew chief and engine builder for Petty Enterprises; he was also crew chief for Pete Hamilton's winning ride in a Petty car, at the 1970 Daytona 500.

## Kyle Petty
### (BORN JUNE 2, 1960)

Kyle, Richard's son, started the 2006 season having made 758 starts in NASCAR NEXTEL Cup, winning 8 races and posting 171 top-ten finishes. Kyle finished fifth in final point standings twice—in 1992 and '93. He was part of an epic 1992 season finale at Atlanta Motor Speedway, in which five drivers started the day with a chance to capture the series championship. That race was also the career finale for his father, Richard. Kyle also has fifty-five starts in the NASCAR Busch Series, and one in the NASCAR Craftsman Truck Series.

## Ritchie Petty
### (BORN JUNE 20, 1968)

Ritchie, Maurice Petty's son, made four starts in NASCAR NEXTEL Cup—three in 1993, one in '94. He also had one NASCAR Craftsman Truck start, in '96.

## Adam Petty
### (JULY 10, 1980-MAY 12, 2000)

Adam, Kyle's son, had forty-three starts in the NASCAR Busch Series between 1998 and 2000. He ran full-time in 1999, with three top-five finishes and four top tens. Adam made two NASCAR Craftsman Truck starts in 1999. His only NASCAR NEXTEL Cup race was April 2, 2000, at Texas Motor Speedway, where he started thirty-third and finished fortieth. That race came three days before the death of his grandfather Lee—and a little more than a month before his own passing.

IN 1959, A DREAM OF NASCAR FOUNDER BILL FRANCE SR. HAD BECOME reality. Daytona International Speedway was ready for racing, a 2.5-mile track with a unique "tri-oval" configuration and daunting 31-degree banking in the turns. On February 22, 1959, the first Daytona 500 was run.

When the checkered flag flew, Johnny Beauchamp was declared the winner. Lee Petty, though, said "Hold on"—or something to that effect. Lee protested, imploring NASCAR to review photos of the three-abreast finish: The lap-down car of Joe Weatherly also crossed the line with Beauchamp and Lee, compounding the confusion.

France listened to Lee, and went about seeking any and all photographic evidence of what really transpired at the stripe. Three days later, France reversed the original call and awarded the victory to Lee.

Lee's son Richard was also in that first 500. He started sixth in the field of fifty-nine—that's right, 59 in '59—and finished fifty-seventh.

LEE WASN'T OPPOSED TO PROTESTING. LATER IN THE 1959 SEASON, Richard learned that all too well. On June 14, at Lakewood Speedway in Atlanta, Richard thought he had the first victory in NASCAR's top series. He was sure of it, in fact. So were most people at the race track. Lee wasn't among them.

When Richard rolled into Victory Lane, his father turned one more lap, then told scorers they had waved the checkered flag a lap prematurely. The stats were checked and Lee was right. Richard settled for second. Lee went on to the series championship that year.

**OPPOSITE**: Lee Petty (right), receiving the Daytona 500 trophy in 1959. **BELOW**: Brochure for the first races at the new Daytona International Speedway, February 1959 (left), where Lee won the first Daytona 500 (below).

CLOCKWISE FROM TOP LEFT: A ticket to the 1974 NASCAR awards banquet—Richard Petty's fifth championship. • A brochure cover featuring Richard's 1967 season—the most successful in history. • A pit pass from the speedway where Lee Petty got his first NASCAR victory in 1949.

RICHARD COULDN'T RACE UNTIL HE WAS TWENTY-one years old. Lee said so, and that, basically, was that.

Richard turned twenty-one on July 2, 1958. On July 18, he entered his first NASCAR NEXTEL Cup event. It was held in Toronto, Canada, at a facility called the Canadian Exposition Stadium. The track was a third of a mile of pavement.

Richard went out, because of an accident, after running fifty-five of a hundred laps. He earned $115.

Lee won the race.

**ABOVE:** Richard Petty's first race at Daytona, 1959. **RIGHT:** A mid-race accident involving both Richard (No. 43) and Lee (No. 42), Martinsville, 1960.

RICHARD'S FINAL VICTORY, NUMBER TWO HUNDRED, may well have been the most memorable of them all, starting with the track where it took place, Daytona International Speedway.

Back then, in 1984, Daytona's July race was still called the Firecracker 400 and it was still held on July 4, no matter what the day of the week, which made for a true holiday atmosphere.

President Ronald Reagan flew in. He didn't make it in time for the start of the race, but since he was, after all, president, they let him give the "Gentlemen, start your engines" command from Air Force One, and it was piped through the public address system.

The president, a former sportscaster and race announcer himself, joined the MRN radio crew in their booth, and actually called a few minutes of the race.

Meanwhile, Richard Petty and Cale Yarborough—with ten series championships between them—were heading toward a rousing finish. On Lap 157 of the 160-lap event, a wreck brought out the caution. Back then, drivers raced back to the stripe after the yellow flag flew, to secure their positions. Richard and Yarborough banged fenders through the backstretch, then through Turns 3 and 4, and into the tri-oval. Richard nudged ahead at the stripe for the milestone victory.

At the time, few could've predicted that victory number two hundred would be the last one for Richard. It's also interesting to note that the win came in a Mike Curb–owned car. After the 1983 season, Petty actually had left the family operation, angered over a late-season rule infraction that resulted in a $35,000 fine. Petty returned to the fold in 1986.

**ABOVE LEFT AND RIGHT:** Richard crosses the finish line and celebrates in victory lane after his 200th—and final—win in 1984. **BELOW:** Bobby Allison and Ronald Reagan (left and center) congratulate Richard, 1984.

ABOVE: Lynda and Richard Petty. OPPOSITE ABOVE: Richard wrecks in his last career start, at Atlanta in 1992. OPPOSITE BELOW: Richard's final Daytona 500 start, 1992.

MUCH WAS HAPPENING ON THE AFTERNOON OF NOVEMBER 15, 1992, at Atlanta Motor Speedway, with the running of the Hooters 500, that season's final NASCAR NEXTEL Cup race. To start, five drivers were still in contention for the series championship. An interesting sidelight was the entry of a young driver named Jeff Gordon, a former open-wheel hotshot who had looked pretty promising in the NASCAR Busch Series.

It was also Richard Petty's final race, a situation that potentially could've overshadowed the championship battle. But ninety-six laps into the event, six cars came crashing into the speedway's front straight. One of them was the No. 43 Pontiac. For a moment, Petty's blue-and-red STP car turned orange as the Pontiac caught fire. Petty climbed out and returned to the garage to oversee two hours of repair work aimed at returning the fabled machine to the track for some late, semiceremonial laps.

"It was just one of them deals," said Petty, with the definitive driver summation. "But if you're going to go out, you might as well go out in a blaze of glory."

The No. 43 did make it back just in time for the final lap. Petty then parked it and walked to another Pontiac, this one a shiny black convertible, in which his wife, Lynda, waited. They rode around for a few more laps and then, after thirty-five seasons, Richard Petty was done.

LEFT: Richard (left) with Bobby Hamilton at Daytona in 1996; a 1992 fan appreciation tour logo. OPPOSITE: (left to right) Three generations of Pettys—Kyle, Lee, and Richard.

1992 FAN APPRECIATION TOUR

RICHARD PETTY

STP 43

I'LL REMEMBER 1958–1992

PETTY ENTERPRISES WAS STRUGGLING long before Richard's retirement, which became apparent as he went winless during his last eight seasons, the last six of those with Petty Enterprises. Starting the 2006 season, the organization hadn't won a NASCAR NEXTEL Cup race since 1999.

But beginning in 2006, there was a renewed effort to reclaim past glories. Bobby Labonte, the 2000 NASCAR NEXTEL Cup champion, was hired as the new driver of the No. 43. Todd Parrott, crew chief for Dale Jarrett's 1999 championship season, was the new crew chief. And former Petty crew chief Robbie Loomis—who was Jeff Gordon's crew chief during a championship season in 2001—had assumed the role of executive vice president of Petty Enterprises.

Whether these recent efforts will resurrect past glory remains to be seen. Regardless, the Petty legacy will surely remain.

# *The* ALLISONS

THE FIGHT.

All these years later, still, it all comes down to that. The Allison name in NASCAR is forever tied to a few rascally minutes between Turns 3 and 4 at Daytona International Speedway, when brothers Bobby and Donnie brawled—sort of—with another NASCAR legend, Cale Yarborough, while a curious nationwide television audience watched.

The actual battle, which has become part of NASCAR lore and likened to Ali-Frazier III at times, in fact lasted all of perhaps thirty seconds. Yet it was a memorable ending to a memorable event—the first time the 500 was televised in its entirety, with CBS doing the honors.

Here's how it developed:

On the last lap of the 500, Donnie Allison and Cale Yarborough were racing down the backstretch, running first and second. Cale dropped low to try to get by, and Donnie of course blocked; after all, the Daytona 500 was at stake. Their cars hit and went flying out of control into the wall in Turn 3, then went spinning and sliding down the banking into the infield grass.

Meanwhile, NASCAR's most prolific champion, Richard Petty, was then able to cruise by and take his sixth Daytona 500 triumph. Incredible as it may seem now, that was almost an afterthought at the time, with Donnie and Yarborough climbing out of their mashed vehicles, apparently headed toward another collision course of sorts.

As Donnie and Yarborough argued, Bobby, on his cool-down lap after an eleventh-place finish, pulled over and began defending his brother, and Yarborough headed in his direction. After a brief give-and-take, Yarborough whacked Bobby in the face with his helmet. That resulted in a description for the ages from Bobby about what happened next:

"I got out of my car and all of a sudden, Cale's nose started beating on my fist."

What was Donnie doing? After a moment or two he and a few track workers tried to separate Bobby and Yarborough. Some photos make it look like it was a three-man brawl, but in reality, it was anything but that. In fact, Donnie never even threw a punch.

Bobby and Cale quickly were separated, but by then history had been made, and was later helped by hype.

But while memories of the 1979 Daytona 500 late-race scuffle sometimes overshadow the family's accomplishments, they also sometimes overshadow other memories, particularly the tragedies that have sorely tested a proud family that once led a great group of racers known as "The Alabama Gang."

Bobby's son Clifford died in 1992 at Michigan International Speedway, after crashing during a NASCAR Busch Series practice session. Bobby's son Davey—a fan favorite and, many said, a future NASCAR NEXTEL Cup champion—died in 1993, after crashing a helicopter in the Talladega Superspeedway infield.

Before his sons passed away, Bobby

ABOVE: Donnie separates Bobby and Cale during their fight at the Daytona 500 in 1979. RIGHT: Bobby Allison's championship car (No. 22, left) at Martinsville, Va. OPPOSITE: Bobby celebrates in Victory Lane with son Davey (left, white shirt) and nephews, Talladega 1971.

himself almost perished after a 1988 accident at Pocono Raceway. It ended his career but not his life, and he went about an arduous and admirable recovery that has, after all these years, elevated him to being one of NASCAR's most beloved former champions—NASCAR royalty, in fact.

In recent years, that tribute and respect has been more obvious than ever: the standing ovations when Bobby appears at a banquet; the three-deep crowd of fans who gather when he's spotted at a race track, walking slowly, limping slightly, through the garages he once ruled.

Bobby Allison, simply, is revered: for what he did, and for what he went through. And also for how he has survived, having gone to hell and back, yet retaining a dignity that honors the memories of his boys as well as his own accomplishments.

Nonetheless, people can't help themselves around Bobby. Inevitably, the question will pop up.

"Bobby, what about that fight?"

Bottom line: It wasn't as bad as it looked.

### Bobby Allison
(BORN DECEMBER 3, 1937)

Bobby has eighty-four NASCAR NEXTEL Cup career victories, tied for third with Darrell Waltrip on the all-time list. In addition to winning the 1983 NASCAR NEXTEL Cup title, he finished second five times (1970, '72, '78, '81, '82). Two especially great periods: a combined twenty-one victories in 1971 and 1972, and thirty-five between 1978 and 1984. Bobby had three Daytona 500 victories (1978, '82, '88). The last victory of his career came in the 1988 Daytona 500. He was named one of NASCAR's 50 Greatest Drivers in 1998.

### Donnie Allison
(BORN SEPTEMBER 7, 1939)

Donnie, Bobby's younger brother, won ten NASCAR NEXTEL Cup races during a career that also saw him chase open-wheel aspirations. That dual effort peaked in May 1970: Donnie won the Coca-Cola 600 in Charlotte, then finished fourth in the Indianapolis 500, six days later. He also had seventeen poles during his career.

### Davey Allison
(FEBRUARY 25, 1961–JULY 13, 1993)

Davey, Bobby's son, had only 191 NASCAR NEXTEL Cup starts, but nineteen of those were wins, with ninety-two top-ten finishes. The 1987 Raybestos Rookie of the Year, he became the first rookie to win two races. Davey made eighty-six starts in the NASCAR Busch Series, but surprisingly never won, despite thirty-one top-ten finishes. He joined his father posthumously on the list of NASCAR's 50 Greatest Drivers, in 1998.

### Clifford Allison
(OCTOBER 20, 1964–AUGUST 13, 1992)

Bobby's younger son, Clifford made twenty-two NASCAR Busch Series starts between 1990 and 1992, with two top tens. Clifford's best finish was sixth, at Bristol Motor Speedway in April 1991.

ABOVE: Donnie and his folks at the Firecracker 400, 1970. RIGHT: Donnie (left) and Bobby, 1971. OPPOSITE: Donnie wins the first Winston-sponsored race, May 1971.

The FAMILY STORIES

LONG BEFORE THE FIGHT, LONG BEFORE THERE WAS AN ALABAMA Gang, there was what you might call a semi-gang, in a semi-city called Hialeah, Florida, a bit northwest of Miami.

Hialeah was a big racing town—if you were talking horse racing. Hialeah Park, which opened in 1925, became a nationally known sporting facility. Suffice it to say that Hialeah Speedway was not nationally known. Neither were the Allisons, nor their buddy Red Farmer, who were all racing, but also spinning their wheels somewhat, anxious to start making their mark in the sport.

Between 1962 and 1964, the three friends packed their families up and headed north. They had heard that there was great racing on paved tracks in Alabama. They found one: Montgomery Motor Speedway. "The place was gorgeous," Bobby recalls.

"We adopted Alabama as our home. It was like you were born at sea, and

you finally found home. I was having a great time, and it seemed Donnie was enjoying it with me." As for competition between the brothers, Donnie says, "The only thing my mother always said is she wanted a dead heat between Bobby and I. And I told her that would never happen because I wouldn't let him win, and I know he wouldn't let me."

But the important thing was, according to Donnie, "We realized we could do what we wanted to do, and still make a living."

Could they ever. The wins came in droves, and eventually, so did a nickname— "The Alabama Gang."

"We thought it sounded so good," Bobby says.

"Our reputation got built pretty quick," adds Donnie.

That reputation followed them, from the short tracks of their adopted home state to NASCAR superspeedways across the land.

CLOCKWISE FROM TOP LEFT: A NASCAR news bulletin stating Donnie and Bobby Allison's one-two finish at Talladega, May 16, 1971. • A Davey Allison trading card distributed by Texaco in 1993. • Bobby's 1983 Grand National Champions bumper sticker.

BOBBY ALLISON'S SOLE NASCAR NEXTEL Cup championship was overdue, to say the least. Coming into the 1983 season, Bobby had been the series runner-up *five* times, one short of Richard Petty's series record of runner-up point finishes. Six victories and twenty-five top-ten finishes brought home the elusive title—barely. Allison clinched in the season finale at Riverside, California, ending up only forty-seven points ahead of Darrell Waltrip.

BOBBY WON THE DAYTONA 500 THREE TIMES, FAIRLY GOOD consolation for his repeated near misses in the series championship chases. Unquestionably, his final 500 win, in 1988, stands as the most historic.

The runner-up finisher that day was his son, Davey. Four years later, after winning the Daytona 500 himself, Davey maintained that his '88 runner-up finish was much more special. And as Bobby recalls, "To win that race at age fifty and to have the best young man in racing be second behind me, and have that young man also be my son, has got to be the greatest achievement anybody could hope for."

Bobby never won another race. Four months later, he crashed at Pocono. For years afterward, he has struggled to regain the memories of that wonderful day at Daytona.

OPPOSITE ABOVE: (left to right) Robert Yates, Gary Nelson, and Bobby Allison celebrate the 1983 NASCAR NEXTEL Cup championship. OPPOSITE BELOW: Bobby wins the 1982 Daytona 500. ABOVE: Bobby showers his son with beer after winning the Daytona 500 in 1988. RIGHT: Davey finishes a close second to his father, Daytona 500, 1988.

BOBBY'S STRUGGLE WAS ESPECIALLY TOUGH THAT FIRST YEAR after the crash. He had indeed lost "patches" of memory. So he was going about, as he told people, to build new memories.

Which made the afternoon of July 1, 1989, emotional, to say the least.

Davey won the Pepsi 400 that day. He was joined for the post-race interview sessions by his father, who addressed his slow recovery, saying that because of his memory loss, he "had plenty of room for new memories," and that he hoped Davey would keep winning, so he could, in effect, "restock" those memory banks.

"I read an article in a magazine," Davey said, "about how someone who'd had a great career in the outdoors had passed along his knowledge to someone younger, and how much joy he got watching that younger person experiencing things for the first time." "New eyes" was the way he put it, that he was watching it all over again and bringing back memories.

"In a way I feel like I'm the new eyes for my dad today."

**ABOVE**: Davey finishes first at the 1989 Pepsi 400 at Daytona. **RIGHT**: Davey drove his dad's Matador (No. 12) at the Daytona in the ARCA series. **OPPOSITE**: Davey with proud parents after his 1992 Daytona 500 victory.

FOURTH ANNUAL
INTERNATIONAL
MOTOR SPORTS
HALL OF FAME

Sunday, December 12, 1993
5:00 P.M. Reception
6:00 P.M. Dinner
8:00 P.M. Awards Ceremony
9:30 P.M. Post Reception

UNOCAL 76
OFFICIAL SPONSOR

INDUCTION CEREMONY

BIRMINGHAM CIVIC CENTER
BALLROOM & CONCERT HALL
BIRMINGHAM, ALABAMA

To attend **The International Motorsports Even**
call: **1-205-362-5002**

**Have a Great Time!**

Mingle and Dine with racing Superstars like Bobby Allison, Davey Alli... Mario Andrett... Baker, Kenny B... Dale Earnhar... Elliott, Tim Flo... Granatelli, Dan... Hurley Haywo... Jarrett, Ned ... JuniorJohnson, Parnelli Jones, Fred Lorenzen, Wally Parks, Richard Petty, Carroll Shelby, ..., Darrell ...er Ward, ...ick and ...ers. Join us ...the 1993

**OPPOSITE**: Bobby with Judy Allison, 1981. **LEFT**: A Motor Sports Hall of Fame flyer announcing the ceremony where Bobby was inducted into the ranks of legendary drivers. **BELOW**: Bobby and Davey Allison's trading cards.

VICTORY LANE
BOBBY ALLISON

VICTORY LANE
DAVEY ALLISON

AN EMOTIONAL, BITTERSWEET FOOTNOTE TO THE ALLISON SAGA IS the fact that Bobby and Judy Allison are husband and wife again. Married for thirty-six years, they divorced in 1996, their bond having weakened during the long grieving process after the deaths of their boys.

Another tragedy brought them back together.

Adam Petty died after an accident at New Hampshire International Speedway in May 2000. Only a few days afterward, Bobby and Judy attended the wedding of Davey's widow, Liz. They talked, and decided to attend young Adam's funeral, to offer emotional support to his parents, Kyle and Pattie.

In the process, they found their own hearts had healed a bit. They talked about the past, and about the future. They talked about a future together. Two weeks after Adam Petty's funeral, Bobby and Judy Allison remarried, a justice of the peace in Bessemer, Alabama, presiding.

1989
Winston Cup Champion

# The WALLACES

RUSTY WALLACE WAS NAMED one of NASCAR's 50 Greatest Drivers in 1998, but to reach that status, he had to first become the greatest driver in his family.

Which wasn't easy. His father, Russ Wallace, was a fine driver, the classic weekend warrior, racing and many times winning at St. Louis–area short tracks. Russ's sons—Rusty, Mike, and Kenny—grew to love watching their father race, and inevitably started racing themselves.

"We just kind of helped Dad along; we grew up in the sport," Rusty said. "Racing is all I knew. I never did get involved in baseball or football like most kids do. I was always in the race car messing around, and it always stayed that way."

**OPPOSITE:** Rusty Wallace wins the 1989 championship. **ABOVE:** Rusty (right) works on his car with crew chief Barry Dodson.

And when he said always, he meant just that—*always*.

Even after he became a NASCAR icon, it was not uncommon to find Rusty out in the garage area under the hood, turning a wrench or telling a mechanic how to. He could talk setups with anyone. When he complained about his car, he always had ideas how to right the situation. He was in effect the last of a breed, a throwback to the days when drivers were hands-on when it came to preparing a race car.

And because of that, when Rusty Wallace spoke, people listened. Though never as outspoken as Darrell Waltrip, he nonetheless had a penchant for public comment about how races were being run—and won. NASCAR rules were

ABOVE: Rusty (left) and Kenny Wallace. OPPOSITE: Kenny after his first career win, Barberville, Florida, 1991.

fair game, and so were NASCAR NEXTEL Cup competitors who had displayed questionable judgment in the heat of battle.

The Wallace brothers helped their dad race, and the all-for-one attitude continued. For years, Kenny served as a crew chief and mechanic for Rusty, as the older brother was moving up the ranks of stock-car racing.

It all peaked in 1991, when all three Wallace brothers raced together in NASCAR NEXTEL Cup—the first time that had happened since the days of the Famous Flocks, nearly forty years before.

Rusty has retired, having won the NASCAR NEXTEL Cup championship in 1989, and has turned his attention to his son Steve's budding career. Kenny and Mike race on.

CLOCKWISE FROM LEFT: Mike (left) and Rusty Wallace at Christmas, circa 1963; Mike Wallace behind the wheel; Steve Wallace. OPPOSITE: Kenny wins his first NASCAR NEXTEL Cup pole, in 2001.

### Kenny Wallace
(BORN AUGUST 23, 1963)

Kenny started the 2006 season with nine victories in the NASCAR Busch Series, but is still seeking his first NASCAR NEXTEL Cup victory. One of the stalwarts in the NASCAR Busch Series, he was the series runner-up in 1991. Kenny finished in the top ten of the final NASCAR Busch Series points five consecutive times between 1989 and 1994. He was the NASCAR Busch Series Rookie of the Year in 1989—the first year the award was given—and started 2006 with twenty-seven top-ten runs in NASCAR NEXTEL Cup.

### Steve Wallace
(BORN AUGUST 18, 1987)

Steve, Rusty's youngest son, made his national series debut at Memphis Motorsports Park on October 22, 2005, finishing fifteenth in a NASCAR Busch Series event. He started 2006 planning on an approximate ten-race NASCAR Busch Series slate, driving a car owned by, appropriately, his father.

### Rusty Wallace
(BORN AUGUST 14, 1956)

Rusty retired following the 2005 season, after a twenty-five-year NASCAR career. He won fifty-five NASCAR NEXTEL Cup races, the eighth-best total all-time. Rusty won the 1989 NASCAR NEXTEL Cup championship, edging Dale Earnhardt by a mere twelve points, the fourth-closest margin in series history. He also finished as series runner-up in 1988 and '93. NASCAR NEXTEL Cup rookie of the year in 1984, Rusty finished his career on a strong note, qualifying for the NASCAR NEXTEL Cup "chase," and ending up eighth in the final points, after having finished outside the top ten at the end of both 2003 and '04. Between 1986 and 2002, he finished the season outside the top ten only once. In 1998, Rusty was named one of NASCAR's 50 Greatest Drivers.

### Mike Wallace
(BORN MARCH 10, 1959)

Mike, like his brothers Rusty and Kenny, has raced in all three of NASCAR's national series—NASCAR NEXTEL Cup, NASCAR Busch Series, and NASCAR Craftsman Truck. He started 2006 with four victories in each of the latter two series, but was still seeking his first NASCAR NEXTEL Cup win. His best seasons have come in the trucks, finishing sixth in the final standings in 1999 and fourth in 2000.

ABOVE: Rusty Wallace, circa 1979. OPPOSITE: Rusty's 1989 championship Pontiac.

The FAMILY STORIES

NOW THAT HIS CAREER IS DONE, IT IS SOMEWHAT HARD TO BELIEVE that Rusty Wallace won only one NASCAR NEXTEL Cup championship. That sole title in 1989, though, was memorable to say the least. Rusty was able to beat the man who, for all practical purposes, has to be held partly responsible for him not winning more championships: Dale Earnhardt.

Granted, it wasn't pretty, the fifteenth-place finish at Atlanta Motor Speedway on November 19. But it was enough to edge Earnhardt—who won the race in dominating fashion—by those precious twelve points.

The Raymond Beadle–owned No. 27 Kodiak Pontiac was only partially compliant on the most important day of Rusty's career. There were two flat tires. A loose lug nut. An errant chassis setup. A vibration problem.

"But that's history now," the new champion said post-race, after making some history of his own.

ABOVE: Kenny Wallace at the Goody's 300 in 1990. OPPOSITE: Kenny leads the 1989 Goody's 300, in which he finished tenth.

THE 1991 SEASON WAS A SPECIAL ONE TO BEGIN WITH FOR RUSTY. It was his first full-time season with legendary team owner Roger Penske and Penske South Racing (he'd driven two races for Penske in 1980), driving cars with Miller Beer sponsorship and the No. 2, both of which would become synonymous with Rusty.

Things got even better during the last two races of the season—at Phoenix International Raceway and Atlanta Motor Speedway. November 3, 1991, was the date at PIR, the Pyroil 500. Rusty finished fifth. Mike was thirty-first, while Kenny finished last, his Pontiac shelved after only one lap because of steering problems.

Two weeks later, at Atlanta Motor Speedway's Hardee's 500, Kenny was the highest-finishing brother, twenty-third, while Rusty and Mike finished thirty-fourth and thirty-ninth, respectively, after crashing.

Historically, those finishes are about as insignificant as it gets, when measured against this: Prior to those two races, the last time three brothers had raced in the same NASCAR NEXTEL Cup event was March 25, 1956, at the old Lakewood Speedway in Atlanta. That afternoon, Bob, Fonty, and Tim Flock all drove in a 100-lap, 100-mile dirt race won by Buck Baker.

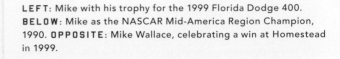

MIKE AND KENNY LONG AGO GAVE UP CHASING THE accomplishments of their older brother, but that hasn't stopped their separate quests for excellence. The night of July 3, 2004, was an excellent one for Mike, as he got his first NASCAR Busch Series victory in more than ten years, and in the process, for the second time, did what Rusty had never done—and never would: win a NASCAR points race at Daytona International Speedway. (Mike also won the 2002 NASCAR Craftsman Truck season opener at Daytona.)

Fate played a huge role in Mike winning the Winn-Dixie 250, a summer Daytona race added to the NASCAR Busch Series schedule in 2002. Both Dale Earnhardt Jr. and Michael Waltrip—then teammates at Dale Earnhardt Inc., who were dominating restrictor-plate races—were involved in separate last-lap incidents with Jason Leffler. Wallace charged through the accidents to win for the first time since August 5, 1994, at Indianapolis Raceway Park.

**LEFT**: The Wallace brothers with their father at Gateway International Raceway in 2005, displaying "Wallace Family Grandstand" plaques. **ABOVE**: The Wallaces take a lap at Gateway International Raceway, 2005. **OPPOSITE**: The Wallace family at their grandstand dedication: (left to right) Kenny, Russ, Mike, Judy, and Rusty.

THE WALLACE FAMILY TRIBUTE 250—THE TITLE OF THE RACE PRETTY much says it all. Held July 30, 2005, at Gateway International Raceway—just outside the brothers' hometown of St. Louis—the event featured all three Wallace brothers on the track, and virtually all of their relatives in the grandstands, including one set of seats that was renamed for the weekend, "The Wallace Family Grandstand."

Mike nearly won the thing—finishing in second place by .710 seconds, behind Reed Sorensen. Kenny finished twenty-fourth, while Rusty wrecked and ended up thirty-seventh.

Results, though, were only part of this story.

The event was mostly a tribute to the soon-to-retire Rusty. He got the key to the city of St. Louis, and obviously was the main fan attraction. But when you honor one Wallace, you really have to honor them all.

"I remember when we grew up in St. Louis," Mike said. "It was a predomi-nantly stick-and-ball sport town. Being race-car drivers or messing with the race cars was not the cool thing to do. I honestly remember our principal and counselors at Fox High School out in Arnold, Missouri, where we grew up, telling us we would never make nothing of ourselves if we kept messing with those race cars.

"Rusty was the first one to set that stage. I'm sure he heard that numerous times himself. To come full circle with Kenny, to have a national race honored in our name, our family's name, in the city that we grew up in, I'm really honored and really happy about the way the whole thing has come down."

Added Rusty: "When we were told, 'We'd like to honor you guys for what you've done,' I was just like blown away."

And, from Kenny: "I grew up watching my brothers Rusty and Mike and my dad work in the garage. We just never did anything else. But I can tell you that I wouldn't trade my family for anything."

# ADDITIONAL FAMILIES

## The Andrettis

Mario Andretti, always fast, flashed across the NASCAR landscape even faster. He was a veritable comet of brilliance. Fourteen races were all NASCAR got out of the man the Associated Press named "Driver of the Century" at the end of 1999.

One of those fourteen was legendary.

The 1967 Daytona 500 was won surprisingly—and with surprising ease—by Mario, who brought a unique, bottom-of-the-track driving approach to Daytona International Speedway's high banks. He won that 500 under a caution flag, but what the record book does not show is the huge lead he had built prior to the caution: more than twenty seconds over his Holman-Moody Ford teammate Fred Lorenzen.

Mario's Daytona triumph came *before* he won the Indianapolis 500 and the Formula One championship. His final NASCAR race came on the Riverside, California,

**OPPOSITE**: Mario Andretti and his 1967 Daytona 500 trophy.
**ABOVE**: John Andretti.

road course on February 1, 1969. The rest of his career was spent chasing his open-wheel dreams. Fans of NASCAR who also were fans of Mario were left to their own dreams of what he could've accomplished in stock cars.

John Andretti is Mario's nephew, the son of Mario's twin brother, Aldo, whose own racing aspirations were curtailed by an accident at a track near the family's home in Nazareth, Pennsylvania, in 1959.

John came into 2006 with 340 NASCAR NEXTEL Cup starts—and two precious wins. One was at Daytona, the 1997 Pepsi 400, in a Ford owned by the famed Cale Yarborough. The other, April 18, 1999, came at Martinsville Speedway, during a period when he had taken over the famed Petty Enterprises No. 43 ride. Coming into the 2006 season, Martinsville stood as the 43's last victory. Also coming into '06, John had a new ride—in the NASCAR Busch Series.

## The Bakers

Buck Baker and his son Buddy—or, to be exact, Elzie Wylie Baker Sr. and Jr.—personified the duality of big-time stock-car racing, where competition and entertainment collide. They were masterful racers on the track and unique personalities off the track, with Buck helping to establish NASCAR's popularity, and Buddy helping to strengthen it.

Buck, who died in 2002 at the age of eighty-three, was one of NASCAR's first great champions. From 1953 to 1960, he never finished the season outside the top five in points. Break that string down a bit more and you'll find a further concentration of excellence: from 1955 to 1958, he was, in order, the series runner-up, the champion for two straight years, and then the runner-up again. The titles won in 1956 and '57 made him the first driver to win the NASCAR NEXTEL Cup crown in consecutive seasons. Buck had forty-six career victories, the thirteenth-best all-time total. His last victory, long past his prime, came in 1964, in the Southern 500, at Darlington Raceway.

The six-foot, six-inch Buddy never won the series championship. He did, however, win nineteen races, including consecutive Coca-Cola 600s in 1972 and 1973 and the Daytona 500 in 1980. After his 699 races in the NASCAR NEXTEL Cup Series, Buddy became a television commentator, and the affable manner that made him a fan favorite as a racer—they called him the "Gentle Giant"—carried over to the screen. Like his father, Buddy was named one of NASCAR's 50 Greatest Drivers in 1998.

Buck's younger son, Randy Baker, also raced, making fourteen starts in NASCAR NEXTEL Cup, and five starts in the NASCAR Busch Series.

After his retirement in 1976, Buck started the Buck Baker Racing School, based at North Carolina Speedway in Rockingham, North Carolina. Buddy and his sister Susie are both instructors at the school. Buck's widow, Susan, is the school's president, while Susie also serves as vice president of operations.

Jeff Andretti, Mario's younger son, made three starts in the NASCAR Craftsman Truck Series in 1999. He has since moved into the business aspect of motorsports.

Michael Andretti, Mario's older son and an open-wheel star himself, has never raced in NASCAR. It remains to be seen whether Marco Andretti, Michael's son, who was an Indy Racing League rookie coming into '06, will make a switch to stock cars someday.

**OPPOSITE**: Buddy (left) and Buck Baker after Buddy's National 500 win at Charlotte in 1967. **ABOVE**: Buddy Baker at Talladega with his children, Bryan and Brandon in 1970.

## The Bodines

The town of Chemung, in upstate New York, is seemingly a most unlikely community to produce not one, but three brothers who would reach the NASCAR NEXTEL Cup Series.

But that's at first glance. Look closer at the Bodine brothers and their saga seems completely natural. Geoffrey, Brett, and Todd Bodine were racers because their father and grandfather built a race track in Chemung.

The Chemung Speedrome exposed the brothers to auto racing at an early age. Geoffrey, in fact, started running laps at the age of five, in a division called Micro Midget.

Three brothers, one collective NASCAR legacy rich with highlights: Geoffrey winning the Daytona 500 in 1986; Brett getting his only NASCAR NEXTEL Cup victory, at North Wilkesboro, in 1990; Geoffrey, in 1998, being named one of NASCAR's 50 Greatest Drivers, in part because of his Modified racing—in '03, he also was named one of NASCAR's top ten Modified drivers of all time.

And then there's Geoffrey, at the age of 52, pulling off a surprise third-place finish in the 2002 Daytona 500, and Todd winning four of the last six in the 2006 NASCAR Craftsman Truck Series season. And Brett joined NASCAR in 2004, as director of cost research, a position aimed at helping contain expenses for competitors.

On the other hand, mention the name Bodine, and ardent NASCAR fans will inevitably think of the 1994 Brickyard 400, when Brett and Geoffrey traded bumps on lap 101, resulting in Geoffrey spinning and the brothers feuding publicly after the race. Then, there's also Geoffrey's dreadful crash in the 2000 truck series season-opening race at Daytona International Speedway. Time has healed both feelings and injuries.

Today, much of the time, Geoffrey is knee-deep in snow—with the U.S. Bobsled Team. Along with Bob Cuneo, with whom Geoffrey has built race cars, Bodine started Bo-Dyn Bobsled Company, which now builds all the sleds used by U.S. teams. At the 2002 Winter Olympics in Salt Lake City, the U.S. team won three medals driving Bo-Dyn bobsleds.

ABOVE: Brett Bodine. BELOW: His brother Todd. OPPOSITE: Geoffrey Bodine celebrates winning the 1986 Daytona 500.

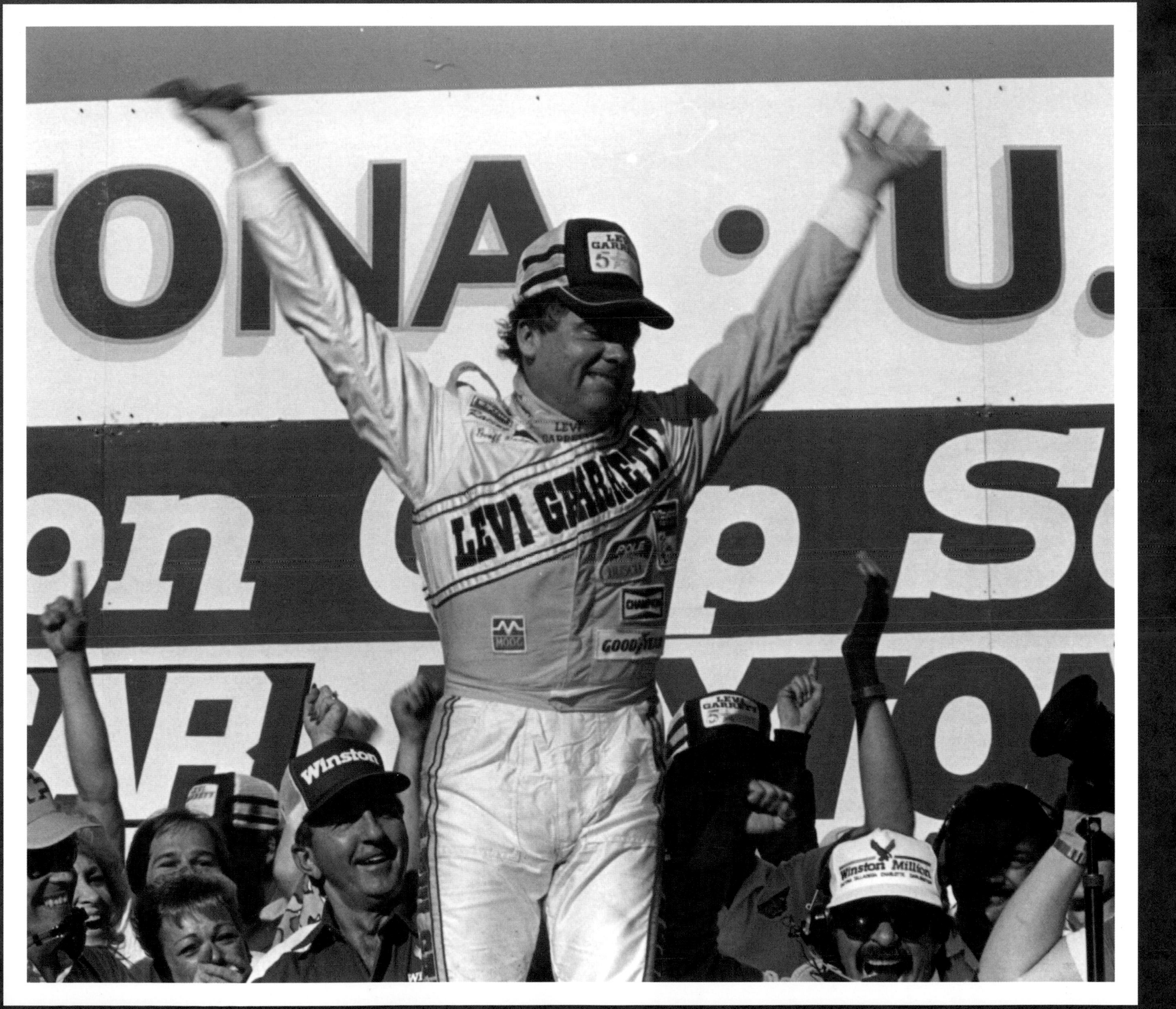
LEVI GARRETT
Winston
Winston Million

Brett is busier than ever, too, working out of NASCAR's state-of-the-art Research and Development Center in Concord, North Carolina, in addition to driving the pace car on NASCAR NEXTEL Cup race days.

Todd, meanwhile, started 2006 chasing the NASCAR Craftsman Truck Series championship, riding the momentum of his 2005 late-season success.

## The Bouchards

Ron Bouchard was the Raybestos Rookie of the Year in 1981 in the NASCAR NEXTEL Cup Series. Ken Bouchard won the same honor in 1988. They remain the *only* siblings to both win Raybestos Rookie of the Year titles in NASCAR's top series.

As for NASCAR NEXTEL Cup race victories, they had only one between them. But what a victory it was.

It happened at Talladega Superspeedway in 1981, years before NASCAR mandated horsepower-reducing carburetor restrictor plates, which meant that racing at approximately two hundred miles per hour was the norm.

Ron won the season's second Talladega race, held in the heat of summer. Some say that the finish was perhaps the greatest in the history of NASCAR: Ron passed two future series champions—Darrell Waltrip and Terry Labonte—in the last quarter mile.

He edged Labonte by less than a yard, and Waltrip by less than a foot.

The Bouchards—from Fitchburg, Massachusetts—both came up through the Modified ranks. Modifieds have long been an extremely popular form of auto racing in the Northeast; some fans in that area follow Modifieds as fervently as NASCAR NEXTEL Cup.

OPPOSITE: Ward (left) and Jeff Burton. ABOVE: Ward Burton. RIGHT: Jeff Burton.

Ron now operates automobile dealerships in the Fitchburg area. Ken works with Ron at the dealerships, and also is involved in a race-driving school at historic Thompson International Speedway, a NASCAR-sanctioned track in Thompson, Connecticut.

## The Burtons

The NASCAR pinnacle for the Burton brothers—Ward and Jeff—of South Boston, thus far? That's easy: Ward winning the 2002 Daytona 500.

It was considered an upset, sort of.

After all, most observers likely would've chosen Jeff as the more likely Burton to win NASCAR's biggest race. In 1994, Jeff was the Raybestos Rookie of the Year in the NASCAR NEXTEL Cup Series. Between 1997 and 2001, Jeff was one of the premier drivers in the sport, with five consecutive years finishing in the final standings' top ten, with a career-high third-place finish in 2000. During that fabulous run, he won several of NASCAR's most historic events—the Southern 500 at Darlington in 1999, the Pepsi 400 at Daytona in 2000, and the Coca-Cola 600 at Charlotte in 1999 and 2001.

That's not to downplay Ward's abilities. In 1999, he was ninth in the

final points, and he finished tenth in 2000. The next year, he also won the Southern 500.

It is a true family tale, this remarkable emergence of two brothers at NASCAR's top competitive level. Their father, John, raced go-karts, and he passed that passion on to his sons. From go-karts, the brothers advanced to the short-track wars staged at South Boston Speedway, which eventually led them to the big time.

Entering the 2006 season, Jeff was helping the storied Richard Childress Racing team's resurgence in NASCAR NEXTEL Cup. Ward, out of competition since 2004, but extremely active with his conservation-aimed Ward Burton Wildlife Foundation, began talking openly in '06 about a return to racing.

## *The Busches*

The Busch Brothers, from Las Vegas, are safe bets to leave separate, lasting legacies in NASCAR.

Big-brother Kurt has a leg up after winning NASCAR's biggest prize, the NASCAR NEXTEL Cup Series championship. That advantage over younger brother Kyle isn't exactly tentative, but by no means is it a sure thing. Kyle was all set to move into NASCAR's Craftsman Truck Series in 2002 at the age of sixteen, before a late-2001, safety-oriented rule change by NASCAR upped the minimum driver age requirement to eighteen.

Kurt, seven years older, won the NASCAR NEXTEL Cup championship in 2004. In 2005, Kyle was the series' Raybestos Rookie of the Year, one year after taking the same honor in America's second-favorite form of motorsports, the NASCAR Busch Series. In '05, Kyle's win at California Speedway—at the age of twenty years, four months, and two days—broke Donald Thomas's fifty-three-year-old record as the youngest NASCAR NEXTEL Cup race winner.

Both started racing in their hometown as teenagers. For Kurt, it was Las Vegas Speedway Park, and Parhump Valley Speedway in Dwarf Cars, then on to Legend Cars and Hobby Stocks. For Kyle, it was Las Vegas Motor Speedway, and Legend Cars.

The Busch Brothers are focused now on building their own legends.

**LEFT**: Kurt Busch holds his 2004 NASCAR NEXTEL Series championship trophy.
**OPPOSITE**: Kyle Busch in 2005.

## The Elliotts

In the beginning, said Bill Elliott, there were no employees, only family members, as he and his brothers sought to carve careers from dreams in Dawsonville, Georgia.

Their race shop was an old elementary school in another rural town, nearby Dahlonega. Their expertise was self-taught, and their race team was self-sufficient. For a number of years, running partial seasons in the NASCAR NEXTEL Cup Series simply had to do.

Bill Elliott was the driver. Ernie Elliott was the engine builder. Both got plenty of help from their other brother, Dan. All three had been steered toward the sport by their father George. They followed the classic grassroots path, initially racing at dirt-track events with piecemeal equipment.

From 1977 to 1981, Bill entered only sixty-five of the 123 NASCAR NEXTEL Cup races run. But he had twenty-three top-ten finishes.

Purchasing some equipment from Roger Penske in the late seventies helped the team's progression. When Bill started running consistently, a man named Harry Melling stepped to the plate and offered the Elliott boys a sponsorship deal starting with 1982. The rest, as the cliché goes, is history.

Bill is semiretired now, his forty-four NASCAR NEXTEL Cup victories fourteenth on the all-time list. He now helps develop drivers for Ray Evernham's Dodge operation, while Ernie is still building engines for other teams.

Coming into 2006, Bill planned on driving in only a handful of NASCAR NEXTEL Cup events. Rest assured that whenever he does run, he'll have plenty of fan support. Between 1983 and 2000, Bill won the NASCAR Most Popular Driver award fifteen times, including ten times consecutively from 1991 to 2000. The award appropriately now bears his name.

He won fans by winning races. Driving Coors-sponsored Ford Thunderbirds that helped redefine aerodynamic packages for both stock and passenger cars, Bill claimed the NASCAR NEXTEL Cup championship in 1988, and finished as series runner-up three other times, including 1985. He didn't win the title that year, but

**OPPOSITE**: Bill Elliott discusses racing strategy with his brother, Dan. **ABOVE**: Bill Elliott explains the handling characteristics of his car to brothers Ernie (left) and Dan.

he nonetheless had one of the greatest seasons in history: eleven victories and a $1 million bonus from the series sponsor at the time, R. J. Reynolds, in a promotion called "The Winston Million."

To win the bonus, a driver had to win at least three of what was then called NASCAR's "big four" events: the Daytona 500 (the richest race); the Coca-Cola 600 at Charlotte (the longest race); the Southern 500 at Darlington (the oldest race); and the Winston 500 at Talladega (the fastest race). Bill won at Daytona and Talladega, then clinched the big payoff by winning the Southern 500.

As a result, Bill became so popular that he required two nicknames. "Awesome Bill from Dawsonville" was supplemented by "Million Dollar Bill."

## The Foyts

A. J. Foyt's fame may be forever linked to the Indianapolis 500, but his reputation owes a nod or two to NASCAR, make no mistake.

After all, Anthony Joseph Foyt Jr., of Houston, did win seven NASCAR NEXTEL Cup Series events, six victories coming while driving for the Wood Brothers—a combination of legends if there ever was one.

Three of those were at Daytona, including his first two: back-to-back wins in the Firecracker 400, in 1964 and 1965. In '72, he reached his NASCAR pinnacle by winning the Daytona 500 in the Wood Brothers' Mercury Cyclone; a month later in Ontario, California, he got his last NASCAR victory.

He also etched his name into NASCAR lore by having his Daytona 500 pole-winning qualifying speed disallowed; inspectors determined his Chevrolet had received an illegal carburetion boost from nitrous oxide.

After 1972, the rough-talking, smooth-driving Texan continued to dabble in stock cars, all the while becoming arguably the greatest of all American open-wheel competitors because of a record four Indy 500 titles. In 1994, after 128 starts, he finally shut it down in the NASCAR NEXTEL Cup Series. Fittingly, the last race was at Indy, in the very first Brickyard 400. He finished thirtieth.

A.J.'s son Larry competed in the NASCAR Busch Series in 2001 and '02, and in the NASCAR NEXTEL Cup in 2003 and '04. Also, grandson A. J. Foyt IV competed in the NASCAR Busch Series in 2005 and '06.

**ABOVE**: A. J. Foyt IV. **RIGHT**: A. J. Foyt with his 1972 Daytona 500 trophy.

LEFT: David (left) and Jeff Green. BELOW: Mark Green.

## The Greens

David and Jeff Green are the only siblings to have both won the NASCAR Busch Series title, a distinction that has earned the Green brothers—David, Jeff, *and* Mark—their rightful status in what has become known as the "Owensboro Posse," a collective label for the various NASCAR drivers who come from Owensboro, Kentucky.

Owensboro, about 150 miles northwest of Nashville, Tennessee, is a town bordered on the north by the Ohio River, and has approximately 75,000 residents. Perhaps Owensboro's most famous residents are the Waltrips, also the Posse's historically dominant family because of Darrell Waltrip's three NASCAR NEXTEL Cup championships, and Michael Waltrip's two Daytona 500 victories.

But the Green boys have done all right, too. David won the NASCAR Busch Series title in 1994, then nearly won it again a couple of other times, finishing as series runner-up in '96 and 2003, the latter by only fourteen points. Jeff was series champion in 2000, a success sandwiched by runner-up seasons in 1999 and 2001.

Coming into the 2006 season, all three brothers were hard at work—David chasing another NASCAR Busch Series crown, Mark also driving in the NASCAR Busch Series, and Jeff driving in NASCAR NEXTEL Cup.

## The Hamiltons

Bobby Hamilton was a champion in 2004. His years of competing at the NASCAR national series level finally paid off, with the NASCAR Craftsman Truck Series title.

His son, Bobby Hamilton Jr., joined him on stage for the emotional celebration at the series' season-ending banquet in Miami Beach, Florida. It was feel-good night for one of NASCAR's most diligent competitors, his family, and friends.

Want to know what NASCAR's all about? It's all about a father finally breaking through and earning national acclaim, with his son—his namesake—at his side, both wearing grins for the ages.

Consider that Bobby Sr. had raced in NASCAR since 1989 without a sniff of a title. Just how special that night was to the Hamilton family, one can only imagine.

Early in 2006, nights like that became even more cherished by the Hamiltons. In March, Bobby Sr. announced he was taking a break from racing to focus on another battle, one against cancer. He also announced that his son would take over his Bobby Hamilton Racing ride in the NASCAR Craftsman Truck Series during his treatments. This announcement had a precedent: When Bobby Sr. left his Morgan-McClure Racing ride in NASCAR NEXTEL Cup in 2001, his son ended up taking over for the last seven races of the season.

For both Hamiltons, the highly competitive truck series has provided a chance to renew careers—and also a reminder, for fans of the Nashville natives, of their considerable talents.

It has also reminded people of how Bobby Sr.'s grandfather, Charles "Preacher" Hamilton, started the family's NASCAR tradition as one of the best car builders around in the 1960s; "Preacher" built cars for country music star Marty Robbins, who also was a pretty good stockcar driver for a number of years.

Bobby Sr. was a NASCAR NEXTEL Cup regular from 1991 to 2002, winning four times. Bobby Jr. drove in the NASCAR Busch Series from 1999 to 2004, winning five times and challenging for the title in 2003, driving for team owner

**ABOVE:** Bobby Hamilton (left), with Richard Petty in 1996. **LEFT:** Bobby Hamilton Jr. with the 2003 Tropicana Twister 300 trophy.

LEFT: Coo Coo (left) and Sterling Marlin.
ABOVE: Coo Coo (in hat), Sterling, and Sterling's son Steadman at the 1994 Daytona 500.

Ed Rensi. He then returned to NASCAR NEXTEL Cup level, with disappointing results that belied his ability.

Entering 2005, the NASCAR Craftsman Truck Series was looking a lot like home for the Hamiltons, a father-son duo increasingly embraced by fans.

## The Marlins

Colorful and competitive. That pretty much sums up the appeal of the Marlins, from Columbia, Tennessee.

It all started with that name: Coo Coo. Unique to say the least, and certainly more catchy than his given name of Clifton, from a promotional point of view. Coo Coo Marlin's racing career spanned five decades—1947 to 1980. From 1966 to 1980, he made 165 starts in the NASCAR NEXTEL Cup Series.

Coo Coo's son, Sterling, was a high school sports star growing up in Columbia. Inevitably, he got the urge to try his father's sport—with his father's support. His mother was against it, but eventually she grudgingly gave in.

Sterling made his NASCAR NEXTEL Cup debut in May 1976 at Nashville Raceway, subbing for his father, who was injured. Thirty years later, he came into the 2006 season with ten career victories.

Two of those ten came as back-to-back victories in NASCAR's premier event, the Daytona 500, in 1994 and '95. That made Marlin one of only three drivers to win the 500 in consecutive seasons; Richard Petty (1973–74) and Cale Yarborough (1983–84) were the others.

But there was something else highly significant about those 500 triumphs. They were Sterling's *first two* in the NASCAR NEXTEL Cup Series. Nothing like breaking through in style.

Fittingly, his father's biggest NASCAR NEXTEL Cup moment also occurred at Daytona International Speedway. In 1973, Coo Coo won the second of two qualifying races for the Daytona 500—the races were then 125 miles in length and called the "Twin 125s." That gave Coo Coo an outside-second-row start; he finished twenty-ninth.

In 1974, he started the 500 thirty-first, but ended up having the dominant car for most of the race. A controversial pit-road penalty relegated Coo Coo to a fourth-place finish.

Coo Coo died August 14, 2005, at the age of seventy-three, and the outpouring of sentiment reminded people of his enduring popularity.

Sterling changed teams prior to 2006, leaving owners Chip Ganassi and Felix Sabates, and moving to MB2 Motorsports, driving Chevrolets with the No. 14 on their sides—the same number his father had.

Sterling's best season thus far was 2002, when he led in NASCAR NEXTEL Cup points for twenty-five weeks, before a neck injury ended his season with seven races remaining.

As Sterling's career winds down, he's helping his son Steadman get his career cranked up. Coming into '06, Steadman had made twenty-three starts in the NASCAR Busch Series and three in the NASCAR Craftsman Truck Series, with total winnings of nearly $400,000.

## *The Parrotts*

In modern-day NASCAR, crew chiefs have become, in some cases, almost as notable as drivers. People like the Parrotts, from Charlotte, North Carolina, are especially deserving of whatever increased recognition the sport's changing landscape brings.

Buddy Parrott and his sons, Todd and Brad, have created a father-son crew chief legacy that has bridged eras. They will be remembered for building championship-contending teams, and for making great drivers even greater.

Buddy never won a championship, surprisingly to say the least, considering his expertise, and the many talented drivers he teamed with. Darrell Waltrip, Buddy Baker, Richard Petty, Rusty Wallace, and Jeff Burton all benefited from Buddy's knowledge.

Forty-four times, Buddy's drivers rolled into Victory Lane in the NASCAR NEXTEL Cup Series; twenty-one of those victories came with Waltrip, between 1977 and '80. Ten other victories came in one tremendous season with Wallace; the series championship challenge was foiled by Dale Earnhardt.

For a while in the 1990s, Buddy had both Todd and his younger son, Brad, working for him at Penske Racing. Eventually the kids left to join Robert Yates Racing; Todd became crew chief for driver Dale Jarrett, who had left the Joe Gibbs Racing operation. In 1999, Todd guided Jarrett to the NASCAR NEXTEL Cup championship.

Entering the 2006 season, Todd stood tall at the helm of the once-proud No. 43 team of Petty Enterprises, one of the key figures in an overall revamping of the Petty operation. The No. 43's new driver, 2000 NASCAR NEXTEL Cup titlist Bobby Labonte, started the year strongly, creating a buzz throughout the sport that the one-time dominant team was rebounding for real.

Brad Parrott, who worked as a crew chief for PPI Motorsports in 2000, was snatched up by the Chip Ganassi–Felix Sabates organization early in the 2006 season, becoming crew chief for driver Casey Mears' partial NASCAR Busch Series schedule.

OPPOSITE: Coo Coo (in car) makes a pit stop while son Sterling (front right) works with the crew. ABOVE: Buddy Parrott. RIGHT: Todd Parrott.

## The Parsons

The "Taxi Cab Driver from Detroit," Benny Parsons, was both affable and accomplished. And there's no doubt that the first quality played into the second.

Fans loved Benny. His racing peers liked him too, which helped him to his two greatest NASCAR achievements.

In 1973, Benny went into the season finale at North Carolina Motor Speedway needing only a respectable finish to clinch the NASCAR NEXTEL Cup championship. But an early-race wreck sent him to the garage, and suddenly a seemingly sure title was in dire jeopardy. Some of his rivals, though, pulled together, with several teams contributing parts and labor to get Benny back onto the race track. They succeeded, and he went on to complete enough laps to finish twenty-eighth and edge Cale Yarborough for the championship.

In 1975, Richard Petty had fallen out of contention at the Daytona 500—so he chose to hook up in a draft with Benny, helping Parsons to run down race leader David Pearson. When Pearson wrecked with two laps remaining, Parsons pounced, and went on to take the victory.

A bit lucky? Perhaps. But in NASCAR, you make your own luck, through your skills, and Benny had plenty, evidenced by his twenty-one NASCAR NEXTEL Cup victories and an incredible nine consecutive seasons (1972 to 1980) of finishing in the top five in the final point standings. Those kinds of stats more than justify his inclusion on the NASCAR's 50 Greatest Drivers list.

Benny's younger brother Phil raced from 1982 to 2001 in both the NASCAR NEXTEL Cup Series and the NASCAR Busch Series. He had one victory at the top level, in the 1988 spring Talladega. In the NASCAR Busch Series he won twice, with spring-race wins at Bristol Motor Speedway in 1982 and at Lowe's Motor Speedway in 1994.

## *The Pembertons*

NASCAR's foundation may have been formed in the Southeast, but in the Northeast there have long been legions of faithful fans and fervent competitors.

People like the Pembertons.

Malta, New York, was home to four Pemberton brothers—Robin, Randy, Ryan, and Roman—and through the years, NASCAR became their love, in part because of an allegiance to one of NASCAR's first stars from the Northeast, Pete Hamilton of Dedham, Massachusetts.

On February 22, 1970, the Pembertons had traveled to Lake Placid, New York, to watch local hockey teams battle. But while the parents were inside the Olympic Center Ice Arena, the boys were sitting in the car, shivering of course, as people do in mid-February in New York.

A static-filled radio broadcast of the Daytona 500 kept them in that car—until their hero Hamilton had taken the checkered flag. Robin remembers running into the arena, shouting, "Pete won the Daytona 500."

Robin calls that day a dream come true.

There were more such days to come.

Robin and Ryan went on to become NASCAR NEXTEL Cup crew chiefs. Robin later became Ford's field representative for all NASCAR NEXTEL Cup teams. In 2005, completing what Robin considers an almost inevitable progression, Robin joined NASCAR itself, becoming vice president of competition. Ryan continues to be a crew chief, for MB2 Motorsports.

Randy became a motorsports media member, while Roman has worked as both a mechanic and spotter at NASCAR's national series level. These days, the Pemberton name has become synonymous with NASCAR.

OPPOSITE LEFT: Benny (left) and Phil Parsons. OPPOSITE RIGHT: Benny Parsons in 1975. ABOVE: Ryan Pemberton. BELOW: Robin Pemberton.

RIGHT: Hermie Sadler is a veteran of the NASCAR Busch Series with two wins and competes occasionally in the NASCAR NEXTEL Cup Series. OPPOSITE: Elliott Sadler made his NASCAR Busch Series debut in 1995, and moved up to the NASCAR NEXTEL Cup Series four years later.

## The Sadlers

A penchant for fried bologna sandwiches and a down-home dialect lifted from *Gone with the Wind* has made Emporia, Virginia, native Elliott Sadler a modern-day NASCAR folk hero. Elliott has also become a top-shelf driver in the NASCAR NEXTEL Cup Series for one of the best teams around, Robert Yates Racing, in one of the most recognizable of cars, the No. 38 M&M's Ford.

Coming into 2006, Elliott had three career victories in NASCAR NEXTEL Cup, and six poles. In 2004, he was one of the ten drivers who qualified for the inaugural Chase for the NASCAR NEXTEL Cup championship shootout; he finished ninth. Prior to coming to NASCAR's top series, Elliott had five victories and five poles in the NASCAR Busch Series.

In all of this, he was following the lead of his older brother Hermie, who finished in the top ten of the final NASCAR Busch Series standings four times between 1993 and 1998, with a career-best fifth-place standing in 1994—and two victories and three poles along the way. Hermie came into 2006 racing part-time in NASCAR NEXTEL Cup, having made fifty-two starts between 1996 and 2005.

Hermie races part-time because his daughter Hailie was diagnosed with autism in 2002, which caused a shift in priorities for the driver. Since his daughter was diagnosed, Hermie and Elliott—joined by many of their peers—have been involved in a number of events to raise funds to benefit autism awareness.

## The Scotts

Wendell Scott's pioneering efforts in NASCAR have received increasing, well-deserved accolades in recent years. Coming into the 2006 season, Wendell, from Danville, Virginia, remained the only African-American driver to win a race in a NASCAR national series. The historic event occurred on December 1, 1963, on a half-mile track in Jacksonville, Florida. That accomplishment and others—such as winning the NASCAR-sanctioned Virginia state Sportsman championship in 1959, and finishing in the NASCAR NEXTEL Cup overall top ten in four consecutive years (1966 to 1969)—were the basis for the movie *Greased Lightning*, in which the late Richard Pryor portrayed Wendell.

**LEFT**: Wendell Scott, No. 11, does battle at Bowman-Gray Stadium in Winston-Salem, N.C. in the late 1950s. **ABOVE**: The Scotts get a car moving in 1962. **OPPOSITE**: (left to right) Wendell Jr., Wendell Sr., and Franklin Scott.

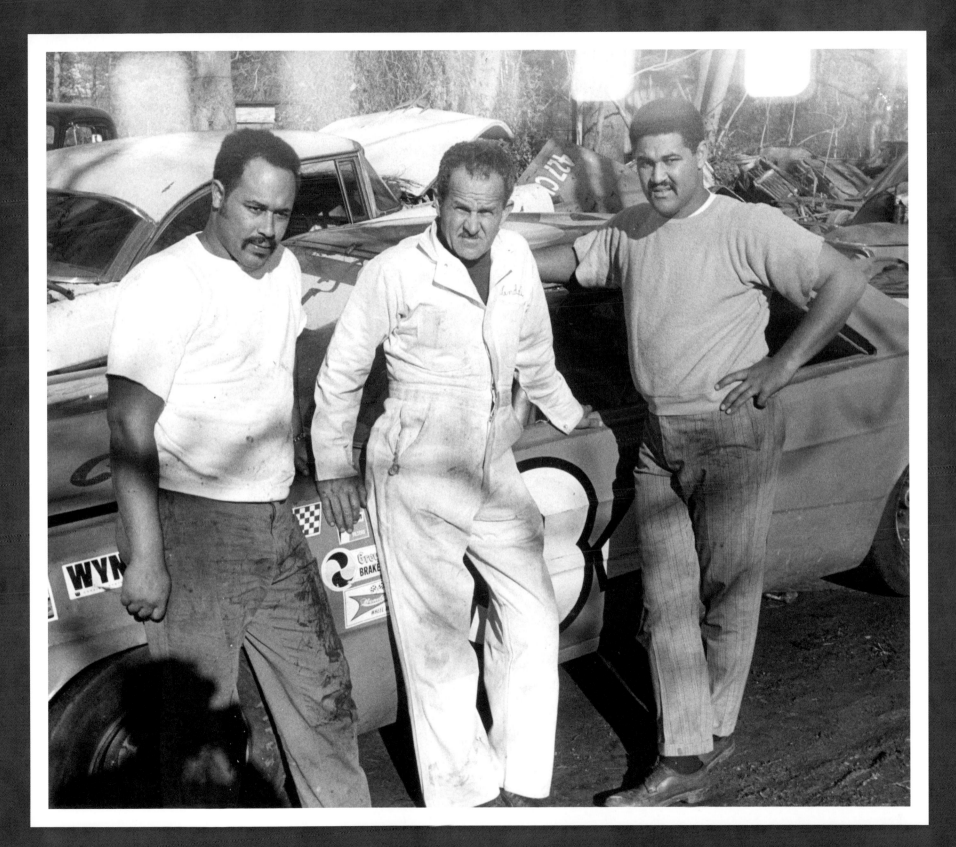

What is especially interesting and endearing is the fact that Wendell's accomplishments resulted from what was truly a family effort. His sons, Wendell Jr. and Frankie, many times served as their father's two-man pit crew. Wendell's wife, Mary, traveled to and from the races as well, serving as the team's "chef," cooking meals that became legendary in the garage area. In addition to her family, she often fed people from other teams.

Wendell and Mary were married forty-six years, their partnership ended only by Wendell's death on December 22, 1990. Today Mary lives in Danville, on Wendell Scott Drive.

Through the years, all six of Wendell's children—Wendell Jr., Frankie, Ann, Deborah, Kay, and Sybil—became regulars at the races.

The times were different, and the times were hard. But for the Scotts, the times were also good, because they were spent together, collectively chasing a dream that lived in the heart of the family's patriarch—and in the souls of his wife and children.

## The Thomases

Herbert Watson Thomas, from Olivia, North Carolina, was perhaps NASCAR's first superstar—with apologies to Freddy Lorenzen and the late Fireball Roberts—as he finished either first or second in the final NASCAR NEXTEL Cup Series points for four consecutive seasons (1951–1954).

Herb won the series championship in 1951 and '53, becoming the series' first two-time titlist. He was also the first three-time Southern 500 winner (1951, '54, and '55).

A racing accident in the autumn of 1956 curtailed his career, but by then Herb already had won 48 races in 230 starts, most driving one of NASCAR's first "super cars," the Hudson Hornet. Herb won 21 percent of his starts, giving him the best all-time winning percentage among drivers with at least a hundred career starts.

Herb's younger brother, Donald, made seventy-nine NASCAR NEXTEL Cup starts from 1950 to 1956. He had only one victory, but it most certainly ranked as a keeper; his 1952 triumph at Lakewood Speedway in Atlanta made him the youngest race winner in series history—twenty years, four months, and six days. That record stood for fifty-three years, until September 2005, when Kyle Busch won at California Speedway at the age of twenty years, four months, and two days.

**OPPOSITE:** Herb Thomas (behind the wheel).
**ABOVE:** Donald Thomas.

OPPOSITE: Speedy (left) and Jimmy Thompson.
LEFT: NASCAR inspector Norris Friel (left) and Bruce Thompson.

## *The Thompsons*

As most modern-day race fans know, Mark Martin's four second-place points finishes in the NASCAR NEXTEL Cup championship have given him the unofficial title of the greatest driver in NASCAR history to have never won the championship. If that were an actual competition, one could state a case for Alfred "Speedy" Thompson being the runner-up.

Thompson, from Monroe, North Carolina, finished third in points not once, twice, or three times—but four times. And in consecutive seasons no less, from 1956 to 1959.

Speedy sped to twenty wins—including the 1957 Southern 500—and nineteen poles, before dying of a heart attack during a NASCAR Sportsman division race in Charlotte, on April 2, 1972, one day before his forty-sixth birthday.

A year earlier, after being out of NASCAR NEXTEL Cup for nine years, Speedy made a great one-race comeback at the World 600. He started ninth and finished sixteenth.

Speedy's brother Jimmy died in 1964, at the age of forty. He had forty-six starts in NASCAR's top series, with nine top-ten finishes.

The Thompson brothers' father, Bruce, was an accomplished mechanic and car owner. His cars made nineteen NASCAR NEXTEL Cup starts, with Speedy, Jimmy, Richard Riley, and Bunk Moore the drivers.

The Thompsons should be remembered as old-time racers who bridged eras, successfully adapting as NASCAR's competitive landscape changed with the times.

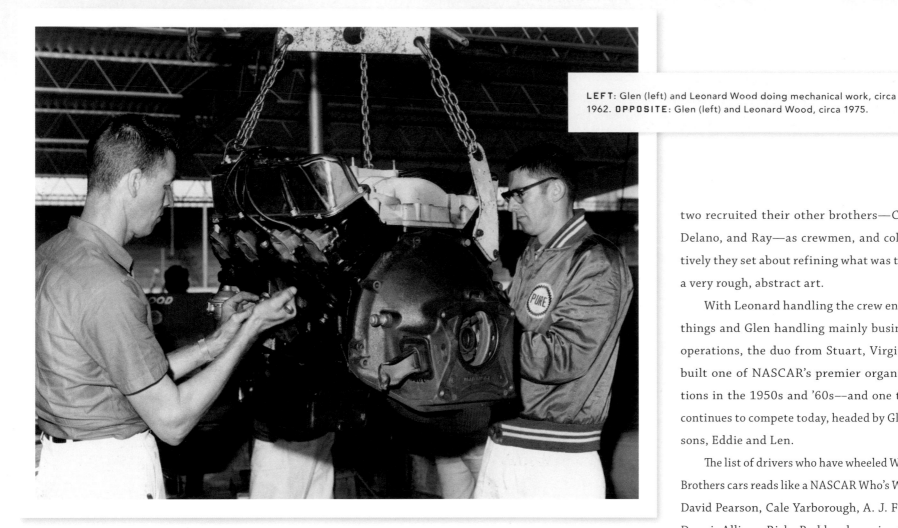

## The Woods

In today's highly competitive NASCAR world, pit stops are vital to a team's success. Seconds, half-seconds—milliseconds, even—add up all too quickly when competing against forty-two other capable crews on pit road.

This wasn't always the case.

In NASCAR's formative years, pitting was seen as necessary, but not particularly crucial to determining victories.

The Wood Brothers changed that.

Leonard Wood became renowned for developing a new type of car jack that needed only several pumps to raise a race car, rather than the fifteen or so required by traditional jacks. But that piece of equipment was only part of an overall, well-oiled machine assembled by Leonard and his brother Glen. Those two recruited their other brothers—Clay, Delano, and Ray—as crewmen, and collectively they set about refining what was then a very rough, abstract art.

With Leonard handling the crew end of things and Glen handling mainly business operations, the duo from Stuart, Virginia, built one of NASCAR's premier organizations in the 1950s and '60s—and one that continues to compete today, headed by Glen's sons, Eddie and Len.

The list of drivers who have wheeled Wood Brothers cars reads like a NASCAR Who's Who: David Pearson, Cale Yarborough, A. J. Foyt, Donnie Allison, Ricky Rudd and, coming into the '06 season, Ken Schrader. Surprisingly, the Wood Brothers have never won the NASCAR NEXTEL Cup title, but it should be noted that for many years they did not compete full-time.

Sometimes overlooked is the fact that Glen Wood was also a great race-car driver—named one of NASCAR's 50 Greatest Drivers, in fact, in 1998. That honor was bestowed because of his success in NASCAR's Sportsman and Modified ranks. Glen did, however, make sixty-two NASCAR NEXTEL Cup starts between 1953 and 1964, winning four times—all at Bowman Gray Stadium in Winston-Salem, North Carolina.

Instilling more life into the Woods' rich legacy is the emergence of Jon Wood, Eddie's son. At the start of 2006, Jon was twenty-four years old and driving full-time in the NASCAR Busch Series. He came to that series after four years in NASCAR Craftsman Truck competition, where he won twice.

**ABOVE:** Richard Petty leads his son Kyle through Turn 4 at Daytona International Speedway in December 1977 during Kyle's first practice session in a stock car. **OPPOSITE:** Tony Stewart, Jimmie Johnson, and Jeff Gordon rumble through Turn 4 at Martinsville Speedway, NASCAR's last charter track. The Virginia oval has been holding NASCAR NEXTEL Cup Series events since 1949.

# *Epilogue*

FAMILIES ARE THE FABRIC OF NASCAR'S PAST, AND THERE'S NO DOUBT that families will help form the sport's future as well.

Family involvement in NASCAR is a source of pride, especially for the family that has guided the sport all these years, the Frances. During a speech in 2005, NASCAR Vice Chairman Bill France Jr. addressed that pride, saying, "It comes from making something from nothing, which is just what my parents—Bill Sr. and Annie B. France—did more than fifty years ago when they founded NASCAR."

Pride, he said, "comes from seeing your parents' dreams regarding NASCAR's growth come to fruition, and knowing you played a part in that. And it comes from seeing your children grow up into fine people who are ready to step in and keep the ball rolling, so to speak."

But Bill Jr. was also quick to spread the credit.

"When I talk about family I can't only talk about the France family. I also have to talk about the NASCAR family, which is nationwide but still close-knit. As you might imagine, I'm pretty proud of that family too."

A sample of the significance of family in NASCAR is displayed in these pages. But it's also displayed on any given race day, in the garage and in the grandstands. In NASCAR, competitors aren't the only ones who hand down the love of the sport to a younger generation.

A younger demographic is increasingly interested in the sport, and recent surveys show that many people are introduced to NASCAR by relatives. But NASCAR insiders have never needed data to confirm the significance of family. People who truly understand the sport know what they see, what they feel: NASCAR is and always has been "a family deal," as Richard Petty might say.

And there's no sign of that changing anytime soon. Children will continue to follow the footsteps of their racing parents, and torches will be passed. Today's champions are writing tomorrow's records, and in the years to come, we'll turn the page to read these names in new chapters of the next NASCAR family album.

# Acknowledgments

As with any work of this sort, there are people to thank for their roles in helping to make it happen.

NASCAR Vice President Jim Hunter made this happen. So did NASCAR's Managing Director of Communications, Ramsey Poston. Ditto for Jennifer White, NASCAR's Senior Manager of Publishing.

The assistance supplied by Eddie Roche at ISC Motorsports Images and Archives was invaluable. Thanks, too, to ISC Publications' Tom Pokorny and Jon "The Scanner" Schreiner.

And then there's Albert "Buz" McKim.

NASCAR historian extraordinaire, Buz is a man loaded with answers and prone to embellishment—exactly the right combination for someone working on a book.

Buz co-authored a previous work with me, *The NASCAR Vault*. This time around he concentrated on the long hours of research needed to find the right images and memorabilia to make *The NASCAR Family Album* work.

Buz's father raced in NASCAR's Sportsman and Modified classes. Buz tried to follow that lead. He was not very good at this. But that led to another path—commercial art. He designed many paint schemes for NASCAR cars during the 1970s. Eventually, his penchant for racing history landed him a position with ISC's archives. From there it was on to NASCAR, where in 2003 he joined the sanctioning body's public relations department as Statistical Services Coordinator.

Buz' fingerprints are all over *The NASCAR Family Album*—literally.

And finally, a well-deserved acknowledgment of an old mentor from another life, who's now gone behind the sun, as they say. Former fellow journalist Tom Ford preached the NASCAR gospel long before it was fashionable among media, and predicted the sport's popularity boom long before it seemed feasible. Tom always touted the stories NASCAR offered. Even more so, he touted the people involved in NASCAR. I guess what I'm getting around to saying, is that I hope he would've thought this book was OK.

Thanks to all.

Cheers,

H. A. Branham

# About the Author

**H. A. Branham** comes by his love of auto racing naturally. He was born in Indianapolis, and lived only a mile away from the city's famed race track.

Prior to becoming a communications manager with the NASCAR NEXTEL Cup Series in 2001, Branham was assistant sports editor at the *Tampa* (Florida) *Tribune*, where he had previously covered auto racing for fifteen years. Branham won several writing awards while at the *Tribune*; in 1997, he was a finalist in the Associated Press Sports Editors (APSE) feature-writing category, with a story that was deemed one of the top ten in the nation that year. He is the author of the 1996 book *Sampras: A Legend in the Works*, which details the career of tennis great Pete Sampras, as well as *The NASCAR Vault*, published in 2004. Branham lives in Ormond Beach, Florida, with his wife Catherine and their four children.

All images and memorabilia are courtesy of Motorsports Images and Archives, used with permission.